IRC's purpose is a simple one. Those who suffer the loss of their freedom have a special claim on those of us who are free. We make no distinction between terror on the left or right—among nationalities, races, religious or private beliefs. We seek especially to help those who not only seek freedom but wish freedom for others as well. They are not the object of our charity. It is we who are in their debt.

——Leo Cherne, chairman emeritus

Flight

Refugees and the Quest for Freedom

▶ ▶ ▶ ▶ ▶ ▶ ▶ ▶ ▶ ▶

The History of the International Rescue Committee

1933–1993

Written by Mark Dawson

NEW YORK

We gratefully acknowledge our indebtedness to Aaron Levenstein's
history of the International Rescue Committee, *Escape to Freedom,*
published in 1983 by Greenwood Press.

Our deepest gratitude is extended to Alton Kastner and Carolyn Lee,
whose tireless efforts resulted in the selection and presentation
of the photographs here displayed.

The photographs on pages 162, 163, and 165 are by Elizabeth Rappaport.

Front cover photograph: Severe famine in 1985 forced
hundreds of thousands of Ethiopians to head toward Sudan in search of food.

Back cover photograph: Hungarians helping one another cross over
the bridge of freedom at Andau, Austria, November 1956.

ISBN 0-9637711-0-8

First Edition

Designed by Laura Lindgren

93 94 95 96 97   10 9 8 7 6 5 4 3 2 1

To the thousands of dedicated IRC staff and volunteers worldwide who,
for sixty years, have served the cause of refugees, human freedom, and dignity,
with courage, bravery, and incredible commitment.
Heroes and heroines all, this labor of love is dedicated to you.
—Robert P. DeVecchi, president

Contents

▶ ▶ ▶ ▶ ▶ ▶ ▶ ▶ ▶ ▶ ▶

A Note from Leo Cherne, Chairman Emeritus

▶ ▶ ▶ ▶ ▶ ▶ ▶ ▶ ▶ ▶

Albert Einstein's appeal to Americans sixty years ago that resulted in the formation of the International Rescue Committee was in response to a new and dreadful era in history. From that moment on, the lives and safety of millions of men, women, and children would depend upon the concern and generosity of others.

Einstein's anticipation of a terror so severe as to cause the flight of thousands was sadly accurate. But even he could not envision a ruthlessness as horrifying as Hitler's. In urging Reinhold Niebuhr and others to gather and form a rescue operation, Einstein was convinced that this effort would be needed for only a limited period of time.

Among the obstacles faced by the American committee in those early days was the reluctance of most people to believe that the horrors being told about the Nazis could possibly be true.

At that time there were no refugee programs, no government agencies designed to assure the safety and asylum of uprooted peoples, no United Nations. The American committee had to find adequate numbers of people to help those suffering the pains of oppression and fascism, and it did so quickly.

Those in the United States who were prepared to provide sanctuary for refugees fleeing Europe were interventionist antitotalitarians. This has remained the defining character of the International Rescue Committee. It determines the agency's sense of its purpose, and it creates the eagerness around which volunteers and staff gather to carry out a mission.

From the beginning IRC saw itself as both a humanitarian agency that helps people in need and an organization that serves as a symbol of political freedom and human dignity.

IRC has always had a great sense of urgency. Throughout its sixty years the agency has more often than not been the first relief operation to arrive on the scene of human catastrophe. This urgency is also felt in the expenditure of resources. There has always been at IRC the sense that monies spent on anything other than direct life-saving assistance were immorally spent.

What began as a temporary emergency rescue operation has become the largest non-sectarian refugee agency in the world. In the sixty years it has been in existence, IRC has responded to an ever-increasing number of refugees fleeing tyranny, war, and starvation.

In its responses to the human misery of refugee crises, the International Rescue Committee has distinguished itself as more than a charity. It is a determined assertion and embodiment of human freedom.

Leo Cherne

Refugees Flee the Nazis:
A Small Band of Americans Respond

▶ ▶ ▶ ▶ ▶ ▶ ▶ ▶ ▶ ▶ ▶

In 1933 Adolf Hitler became chancellor of the German Reich. In 1933 the International Rescue Committee was born.

The committee arose out of a need. A need to protect not only thousands of individuals threatened by Nazism but freedom itself. The world had known refugees long before 1933. But the ascendancy of Hitler threatened basic tenets of liberty and humanity. Something terrifying had been unleashed. And those targeted for death had to be rescued.

Already in 1931, as the Nazis were undermining freedom, the International Relief Association (IRA), headed by Albert Einstein, was assisting opponents of Hitler in Europe. Two years later, at Einstein's request, a small group of people met in New York City to found the American branch of the IRA. Out of their commitment would come the International Rescue Committee.

The founders included John Dewey, the philosopher and educator; Reinhold Niebuhr, America's foremost Protestant theologian; Bryn Hovde, who later helped to establish the New School for Social Research; and Amos Pinchot, an attorney who served as chair of the group. Other prominent citizens, such as Eleanor Roosevelt, soon joined the effort.

Their mission was clear: to help anti-Nazis escape imminent danger. From a one-room office in lower Manhattan, this group broadened European contacts, solicited financial support, devised routes of escape, and raised public awareness about those they hoped to help.

As Hitler marched across Europe, people fled in all directions. They did not necessarily know where they were going or how they were going to get there. They

THE NEW YORK TIMES
MONDAY, JULY 24, 1933.

NEW GERMAN RELIEF UNIT.

American Branch Formed to Aid Work Headed by Einstein.

At the request of the International Relief Association, headed by Albert Einstein, an American committee has been formed to assist Germans suffering from the policies of the Hitler régime.

Funds are being solicited to send to Mayor Charles Hueber of Strassbourg, in Alsace, France, who is treasurer of the European organization of the International Relief Association. The headquarters of the American committee, of which Amos Pinchot is chairman, is at 11 West 42d Street.

The association has been in existence for the last two years. It aids victims of civil oppression in many lands without reference to religious or political faith.

An emergency session here of the national executive committee of the American Jewish Congress was summoned yesterday for Aug. 6 by Dr. Joseph Tenenbaum, its chairman, to formulate a coordinated plan of action in behalf of the Jews of Germany.

Adolf Hitler seized control of Germany in January 1933.

ABOVE, LEFT:

In July 1933 IRC was founded at the request of Albert Einstein.

ABOVE, RIGHT:

Reinhold Niebuhr, the noted American theologian and humanist, was among the founders of IRC and later became chairman.

RIGHT:

Nazi stormtroopers march into Czechoslovakia in 1938.

knew only that they had to flee or lose their lives.

Many in flight reached a place of safety only to have it become a place of terror as fascism extended its reach. What began as a trickle of refugees became a torrent. Religious groups rallied to support like-minded followers. But independent political, intellectual, and cultural activists with no allegiance to any ideology had no one to befriend them in their fight for liberty.

In 1936 Hitler began devouring Europe "course by course," as Sir Winston Churchill described it. Nazi troops marched into the Rhineland, swallowed Austria, then took Czechoslovakia. With each advance, the refugee tide swelled. The crisis was compounded as people fled fascist Italy and Franco's Spain. Next was Poland, then France.

The fall of France in 1940 finally awakened the conscience of many Americans. French marshal Philippe Pétain agreed to an armistice with Hitler in the "unoccupied zone" headquartered in Vichy, signing away the lives of thousands: Czechs, Italians, Spaniards, Poles, and anyone the Nazis decided was "German."

Intellectuals, political activists, and artists were among the first targeted for death. These high-profile persons were also the first to be assisted by the small band of concerned Americans. It was becoming clear that the committee's efforts had to be expanded. A large-scale rescue operation was needed.

Thousands of children were among the refugees escaping from Spain to France in the wake of the Spanish Civil War who were assisted by IRC during 1938 and 1939.

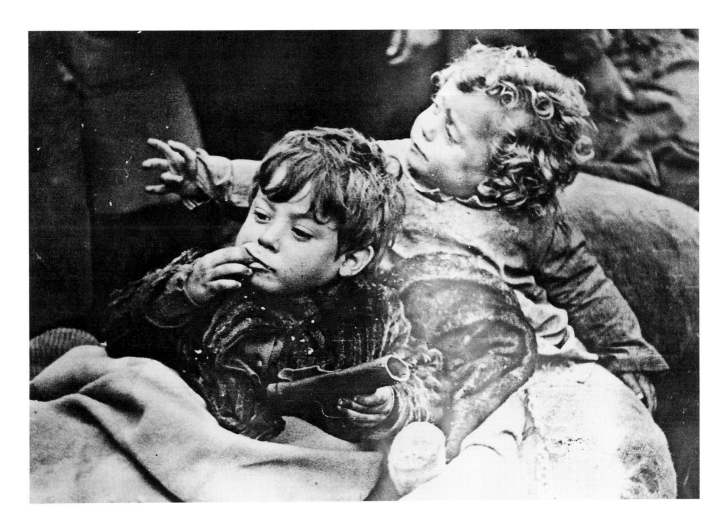

The Marseille Operation

▷ ▷ ▷ ▷ ▷ ▷ ▷ ▷ ▷ ▷

Soon after the invasion of France in 1940, the Emergency Rescue Committee (ERC) was formed to protect the intellectual, cultural, scientific, and political leaders of Europe trapped in Vichy France. The ERC, joined by the International Relief Association, already in France, needed someone to orchestrate a rescue operation.

The person selected, Varian Fry, was a most unlikely candidate. Years later, one of Fry's colleagues in France commented: "Fry's innocence was his great advantage. A more sophisticated man would not have dared to undertake the tasks he carried out so successfully."

A young, bookish journalist, Fry knew several different languages, including French, but had few other qualifications that seemed to prepare him for his mission. Nevertheless, he agreed to leave for Marseille with $3,000 in cash strapped to one of his legs and a list of artists and intellectuals who had to get out of Europe soon if they were to escape certain death.

In France, Fry worked with Carel Sternberg, a young Czech law student who had fled Paris on a bicycle just ahead of the German army. Already a part of the IRA, he quickly became a central player in the Marseille Operation. For Carel this was the beginning of a life-long association with what was to become the International Rescue Committee.

For the small band of rescuers with limited resources, choosing who to assist in the beginning was a daunting task. An advisory committee of Europeans, including Thomas Mann, Jacques Maritain, and Jan Masaryk, was formed to help the committee. Alfred H. Barr, Jr., director of the Museum of Modern Art in New York City, provided the names and where-abouts of artists and helped raise funds for the cause.

Many ruses were used to carry out rescues. At the Hôtel Splendide in Marseille, Fry set up the Centre Americain de Secours, ostensibly a relief agency distributing food and milk. Among the refugee community, however, the real mission of Varian Fry was well known. Hundreds of refugees made their way to his door.

Papers were forged, not always successfully. Sometimes the police cooperated with Fry and warned of impending arrests, but other times Vichy agents betrayed the cause. Many refugees pretending to be French soldiers on their way to North Africa slipped past the Nazis, but many sure-fire escape plans failed.

Over a period of thirteen months the ERC saved at least two thousand individuals marked for death by the Nazis. The primary route of escape was over the Pyrenees, through Spain and

In 1940, as Nazi invaders occupied France, tens of thousands of refugees from all over Europe fled south toward Marseille.

Portugal to Lisbon, then across the sea to America.

Among those rescued were the political scientist Hannah Arendt, artists Marc Chagall and Max Ernst, Nobel Prize–winning biochemist Otto Meyerhoff, harpsichordist Wanda Landowska, novelist Heinrich Mann, and Alma Mahler Gropius Werfel.

Werfel and her husband, Franz, the author, took the same route as many of those who surreptitiously made their way out of Europe. They avoided well-traveled roads, cut through underbrush, and bypassed densely inhabited areas. Arriving in Spain, they were unsure of the reception they might receive.

With them was Thomas Mann's son Golo, who was the only one among their group questioned by the armed sentries stationed along the Spanish border. His papers included an entry visa for the United States, where he was to meet his father at Princeton University.

"So you are the son of Thomas Mann?" asked the sentry.

ABOVE:

Varian Fry at the Marseille Operation headquarters in the Hôtel Splendide.

RIGHT:

Varian Fry (right), who headed the Emergency Rescue Committee (ERC) in France, with Marc Chagall, one of the refugee artists saved from the Gestapo.

World-renowned harpsichordist Wanda Landowska and the writer Franz Werfel (The Song of Bernadette) were among the European cultural and intellectual leaders rescued by the ERC.

"Yes," answered Golo, uncertain of his fate and aware of the presence of Gestapo agents in Spain. "Does that displease you?"

"On the contrary," answered the sentry. "I am honored to make the acquaintance of the son of so great a man."

Then, to the astonishment of all, the sentry telephoned for a car to take the entire group down the mountainside.

Alma Werfel escaped with more than her life. In her knapsack was her husband's draft manuscript of *The Song of Bernadette* as well as the original score of Anton Bruckner's Third Symphony.

Many of those who were warned of impending danger were at first unwilling to believe the Nazis would descend to the depths of inhumanity they did. Rudolph Breitscheid and Rudolf Hilferding, leaders of the German Social Democrats, argued that their worldwide reputations as political leaders would protect

The great sculptor Jacques Lipchitz was rescued from Nazi extermination in France and brought to the United States. His dramatic sculpture Flight *(facing page) is in the collection of the Museum of Modern Art.*

them. Fry pleaded, but they refused to go. When sympathetic Vichy police got word to Fry that both leaders were on "the list," Breitscheid and Hilferding finally agreed to leave. It was too late. They both died by Nazi hands.

Understandably, many others were reluctant to leave their homelands. The Russian artist Marc Chagall, for example, believed he was immune to arrest because he was a naturalized French citizen. When the Vichy government adopted anti-Jewish laws, however, Chagall, the painter of many rural scenes, inquired whether there were cows in America.

When he learned that cows did indeed exist in America, he at last consented to being rescued.

One who did not make it to freedom was Bill Freier, a gifted Austrian cartoonist. He joined Fry's efforts, using his skills as an illustrator to forge identity cards. He also provided a great deal of levity with his clever caricatures of Fry and others involved in the operation. Freier was eventually captured and deported to Poland, where he was killed.

A young anti-Nazi who had fought in the French army against the Nazis volunteered to help Fry. Although in great personal danger, he roamed the Spanish border looking for ways of passage. German-born but easily mistaken for French, he became the committee's chief negotiator with the underworld, bringing back every possible franc for every American dollar and acquiring much-needed but hard-to-come-by services. Not until the Vichy police came searching for him did he agree to flee, using one of the routes he had mapped out for so many others. This volunteer was Albert O. Hirschman, who eventually became an eminent professor of international economic relations at Columbia University.

Despite Hitler's Gestapo, the Marseille Operation was amazingly successful. The cultural and intellectual life of the Western world owes much to the valiant work of Varian Fry and the Emergency Rescue Committee. He and his remarkable band of compatriots did much to thwart the destructive campaign launched by Adolf Hitler. The world has benefited from the creative and accomplished individuals who owe their lives to the rescue mission set up in the Hôtel Splendide. How different it would be had we never known their contributions. Countless individuals whose names we will never know were also saved from certain death.

Inevitably the Vichy government learned of Fry's efforts. His office was periodically raided. During a visit to Marseille by Pétain, Fry and his colleagues were picked up along with other antifascists. For several days they were held on a ship, until the French marshal had departed. Several times Fry was warned of his own imminent arrest, yet he remained in France. There was too much unfinished business. Even when the American consulate urged him to depart, having learned that the Gestapo was putting pressure on the French government to arrest him, he still refused to leave. Finally, in August 1941, he was escorted out of France into Spain. Even then he did not return to the safety of his homeland. Fry spent six more months in Lisbon devising escape routes.

On June 2, 1942, the ERC office in Marseille was raided and closed. Many of Fry's staff in France went underground. Many joined the French resistance movement. The routes of escape established by Fry became avenues for maintaining contact with those still fighting tyranny behind enemy lines.

Two taproots, the International Relief Association and the Emergency Rescue Committee, joined forces in 1942 under the name the International Relief and Rescue Committee, later shortened to the International Rescue Committee. The distinguished historian Charles A. Beard agreed to serve as honorary chairman, and educator Dr. Frank Kingdon served as chairman. The IRC board of directors also included the philosopher John Dewey, college presidents Harry Gideonese and William Allan Neilson, and foreign correspondent and columnist Dorothy Thompson.

What happened in Marseille did much to shape the International Rescue Committee. IRC's mission remains today what it was during the early years: to help those forced to flee persecution and violence. The belief, manifest in Varian Fry, that every life has dignity and is worth saving remains the foundation of the International Rescue Committee.

The Aftermath of War

▶ ▶ ▶ ▶ ▶ ▶ ▶ ▶ ▶ ▶ ▶

The liberation of Paris in 1944 brought much jubilation. It also revealed to the world a city crowded with people uprooted by the war. Soon after France was once again free, the International Rescue Committee opened an office in Paris.

The collapse of the German Reich in 1945 brought chaos. Hitler's vise-grip had been loosened, but the Soviet Union continued to strive for control of all of Europe through military might. Millions of refugees were in need of help. Clearly a permanent agency was needed.

Sir Winston Churchill, in his now-famous speech delivered in Fulton, Missouri, on March 5, 1946, declared:

> *From Stettin in the Baltic to Trieste in the Adriatic, an iron curtain has descended across the Continent. Behind that line lie all the capitals of the ancient states of central and eastern Europe: Warsaw, Berlin, Prague, Vienna, Budapest, Belgrade, Bucharest, and Sofia. Our difficulties and dangers will not be removed by closing our eyes to them. They will not be removed by mere waiting to see what happens; nor will they be removed by a policy of appeasement.*

Many behind that line voted with their feet by refusing to remain in or return to homelands behind the Iron Curtain. Refugees fled to free zones in Germany and Austria. IRC volunteers were among the first to reach the displaced with assistance. Offices were established in Paris, Vienna, Munich, and Rome. A home for sick and aged refugees was set up in Adelboden, Switzerland.

In 1948 the takeover of Prague sounded a death knell for democracy in Eastern Europe that was heard in Poland, Bulgaria, Romania, Albania, and, finally, in Hungary, where the last freely elected parliament in Eastern Europe was supplanted by a Soviet regime. Mass arrests, torture and killing, and concen-

". . . an iron curtain has descended across the Continent. Behind that line lie all the capitals of the ancient states of central and eastern Europe." —Winston Churchill, March 5, 1946

Carel Sternberg (far left), a Czech refugee who joined the IRC staff in 1945, went to Europe after World War II to organize the relief programs for displaced people and refugees.

The collection and distribution of food was a major component of relief work in Berlin.

tration camps became commonplace. Again and again those seeking freedom took flight. IRC provided emergency relief to thousands of refugees and helped thousands more resettle in places offering asylum.

In the spring of 1950 the Soviets called for a mass youth demonstration to convene in East Berlin and then stampede West Berlin. The Communists hoped to overrun the city, crushing its independence. But West Berlin's mayor, Ernst Reuter, moved first. He called for a May Day rally to celebrate the city's freedom, a demonstration that took place in full view of East Berlin's Communist leaders. Reuter also moved quickly to assure that his city would not be cut off from the world and so starved into submission. He called for help from the free world.

IRC initiated Project Berlin, under the leadership of Admiral Richard E. Byrd and General Lucius D. Clay. The American people were asked to open their pockets. Many U.S. citizens, frustrated by an inability to play a direct role in the cold war, saw this as an opportunity to participate. They responded generously with hundreds of gifts ranging from less than $5 to donations as large as $2,500. Every contribution counted: 4,424,000 pounds of milk, butter, and cheese were sent to Europe. The people of West Berlin greeted the deliveries with cheers of gratitude, not only for the provisions but also for America's support of their struggle against oppression. Mayor Reuter remarked: "The American people are united in their will to support the brave people of Berlin in their long and hard fight to remain free."

Stalin persisted in his campaign of terror, jailing and executing people in central Europe and the Balkans. East Berliners were conscripted for his police forces. Citizens who lived near the border of the western zone of the city were pushed farther east. A constant flow of refugees struggled to make their way to West Berlin, the gateway to freedom. By the summer of 1952 the rate had reached a thousand per day. Free Berlin, the beacon of democracy behind the Iron Curtain, remained a thorn in the side of the Soviets.

By early 1953 the burden of caring for this influx of people became too great for one city to bear. Mayor Reuter appealed for help. The IRC board of directors asked its chairman, Leo Cherne, to go to Berlin. Reuter already had a relationship with IRC. He had been director of the IRC office in Ankara, Turkey, immediately following the war. When he had returned to his home city he had been elected mayor.

Upon meeting with Reuter it was agreed that the mayor should come to the United States to plead his case. IRC offered to

In March 1953 Mayor Ernst Reuter of West Berlin (right) came to the United States at the invitation of IRC chairman Leo Cherne (left). They met with President Dwight D. Eisenhower, who supported the IRC campaign on behalf of refugees fleeing Communism.

In June 1953, three months after Stalin's death, East Berliners rose up against Communist rule. Soviet forces crushed the rebellion, creating new waves of escapees.

spearhead this campaign to provide food and other supplies desperately needed in West Berlin. Over a two-week period Mayor Reuter met with President Eisenhower and congressional leaders and traveled from coast to coast addressing large audiences of interested listeners. A special Ernst Reuter Fund was established, to meet the needs of the immediate emergency and to set aside funds for future refugee crises.

In 1951 IRC chairman Reinhold Niebuhr decided to step down. He turned to Leo

Cherne, who since 1946 had been an active member of the board of directors. Cherne accepted, beginning forty years of service as chairman of the board of the International Rescue Committee.

On March 5, 1953, a bulletin from the Kremlin announced that Joseph Stalin was dead. Soon East Berliners mounted a heroic effort to regain their freedom. Nikita Khrushchev, sensing the serious damage being done to Communist rule, instituted a redefection campaign to lure expatriates back home. IRC responded by exposing the campaign's techniques of blackmail, threats, and killings.

Refugees continued to flee. In August 1961 the Berlin Wall was erected. The flow abated but did not stop. The people's longing for freedom could not be subdued by a wall. Women jumped from windows, young people swam canals and rivers, truck drivers drove through concrete, and workers tunneled under the wall. Even some Communist police on sentry duty dropped their guns and leaped to freedom.

Elsewhere along the grim and guarded Iron Curtain, refugees from other Soviet-dominated countries sought ways of penetrating concrete and barbed wire. Alone, in pairs, with families, as groups, they fled.

Relief and health care programs were established by IRC at German and Austrian aid centers. Students were helped with scholarships. In Trieste, Nuremberg, Vienna, and Paris, clothing depots were set up. Exiles were helped to survive, integrate into new settings, and get back on their feet in new lands.

The Fight for Freedom Erupts in Hungary

▶ ▶ ▶ ▶ ▶ ▶ ▶ ▶ ▶ ▶

WE ARE PREPARING FOR TRAGIC POSSIBILITY SOVIET RECAPTURE CONTROL OF HUNGARY, WHEN COUNTLESS ESCAPEES WILL FLOOD INTO AUSTRIA AND THUS MUST BE READY WITH RESOURCES.

So read a cable sent from Vienna by IRC chairman Leo Cherne and IRC president Angier Biddle Duke on October 30, 1956, to IRC headquarters in New York.

A week earlier, on October 23, Hungarian workers, students, and intellectuals publicly proclaimed their desire to be free by staging a peaceful demonstration in Budapest. Two thousand marchers made their way to historic Parliament Square. These quiet but earnest freedom seekers were fired upon by secret police. The demonstrators responded with revolt. The Red Army intervened but failed to crush the movement and withdrew from Budapest.

By then Cherne and Duke had made their way to Vienna, carrying with them the first installment of American aid: antibiotics for the wounded and sick. From Vienna, Leo Cherne and the director of IRC's Vienna office, Marcel Faust, crossed the border into Hungary in a battered Chevrolet loaded with medical supplies. Their destination was Budapest. They were the first Americans to arrive with aid and the first to greet Jozsef Cardinal Mindszenty on his liberation from a Communist prison, where he had been held since 1948 because of his anti-Communist beliefs.

Cherne's notes from those first days in Budapest reveal the faces of the revolution. "What is a revolution?" he wrote.

It is a twelve-year-old boy who sits behind a machine gun nest outside of freedom headquarters for six days.

It is the commandant of a large battalion of freedom fighters who sits at a desk handing out small slips of mimeographed paper with handwritten battle-station orders to an endless line of students and youngsters and workers who pass before that desk. This officer was a young woman who three days later was dead.

The revolution is the harrowed and grateful expression on Cardinal Mindszenty's face as you present to him a gift of Terramycin from the American people. It is the incredible sight of thirty strong, healthy men in worn workers' clothing, each carrying one loaf of bread from your car into the headquarters of the Social Democratic Party as though each loaf was the Hapsburg crown jewels.

Thirty hours later, having deposited the vital supplies with which the car had been filled, having established contact with the leaders of the long-suppressed democratic parties through whom you had

Hungarian freedom fighters storm secret police headquarters in Budapest, where democratic-minded patriots were being held.

hoped to continue to feed very much larger shipments, you learn that the Russians are returning to the city in force. The sound of gunfire becomes louder. The roads outside of Budapest have been closed and you make your way through back roads, no roads, back, back to a world whose faith has been changed by the events in Budapest, whose hopes and whose future have been born again in Budapest.

You rush to the United States to tell the American people that the revolution you have just seen in Hungary is our revolution—the revolution of all who live in the free world. But the American people already know. In large cities, in tiny communities, citizens have banded together to send help. The conscience of America is moved.

The International Rescue Committee was at the vanguard of the rescue operation, and the urgency of the mission was clear. Angier Duke remained in Vienna, organizing the machinery

Proud freedom fighters with the banner that symbolized their struggle for a democratic country.

A FORTUITOUS BREAKFAST

The young American businessman was sitting in a café in Vienna with his wife and a friend, enjoying the quiet of a holiday. It was 1956. Suddenly the peace of the morning was interrupted by the outburst of a young, disheveled man who came flying through the front doors of the café. He rushed to the table and began pouring out his story and that of thousands like him.

Hungary was erupting. Those demanding freedom were being crushed by Soviet tanks. The young man had just escaped in a small boat that carried him across the river along the Hungary-Austria border. Hundreds of young people just like him had been chased into the hills of Hungary to hide. They were being pursued and, once located, slaughtered.

The man pleaded for help. What he wanted most of all were radios to be used by the freedom fighters ever on the move throughout the "hills of resistance," and motors for the boats that would carry away those forced to flee to freedom.

All those who witnessed the event were caught up in the young man's impassioned plea for help.

The American businessman cut short his holiday and returned to the United States. He used whatever friends and influence he could to schedule meetings with targeted corporate executives. In a matter of days he had secured commitments of radios from RCA, motors from Outboard Motor Company, and free transportation from Pan American Airlines.

Soon the young American was headed for Vienna on a plane loaded with radios and motors for boats—vital equipment for those waging a war against oppression. Upon arrival the friend he had shared breakfast with on that fateful morning greeted him. He had a convoy of trucks ready to carry the supplies to the river where they were ferried across to Hungary.

Upon returning to the United States the young American realized that everything he had just arranged had been illegal and that he had interfered with U.S. foreign policy. He went to Washington to "confess" to the CIA, where he was criticized and reprimanded.

Clearly he had been caught up in the events of the day and had done what needed to be done as quickly as possible. In a conversation with a friend about recent events and his concern for the Hungarian freedom fighters, the young American was told about the International Rescue Committee. He promptly investigated this agency and soon found himself a member of its board of directors.

The rest, as they say, is history. Today he is chairman of the IRC. His name is John C. Whitehead.

Over the years John Whitehead has visited virtually every refugee program of the International Rescue Committee. He has, he says, always been impressed with the remarkable courage and bravery of refugees—true survivors willing to risk all for freedom.

▷ ▷ ▷ ▷

for refugee assistance, while Cherne returned to the United States to raise funds. Within sixty days $2,500,000 had been collected from the American public, $357,000 of which materialized following a passionate appearance by Cherne on "The Ed Sullivan Show."

On November 4 the Red Army moved again. The people of Budapest fought back hard and long enough to allow thousands to escape across the border into Austria. Soon Budapest had been recaptured, hastening the exodus of thousands more. Before the Soviets could mend the slash in the Iron Curtain, close to two hundred thousand Hungarians had fled. Many of those fleeing were young

people who feared deportation to Siberia. Young children unaccompanied by parents carried written pleas that families be found to care for them: "Please take care of our child. We remain behind to fight to the last. God bless you."

The vast majority of Hungarian refugees swarmed into Austria. One group headed for the Netherlands and was met at the border by the Dutch Philharmonic Orchestra playing strains of the Hungarian National Anthem.

An episode involving a woman whose name is lost to history reveals the tenacity of people who desire liberty. Near the bridge at Andau, in freezing rain, IRC volunteers

The famous bridge at Andau over which thousands of Hungarians made their way to Austria after Soviet tanks and troops crushed the revolution.

Citizens like General William Donovan, Claiborne Pell, John Whitehead, James Michener, and John Richardson tore themselves away from their immediate responsibilities and headed to Hungary. Other volunteers rushed to help with IRC's rescue mission. Among them was Paul Heber, a Hungarian-born American psychologist. On his first trip to the border Heber said he saw "scores of people struggling across the city waters on flimsy straw rafts. One look and I knew what was needed, a rubber boat." A boat was soon added to the list of purchases made by IRC. On some nights as many as three hundred Hungarians were carried to freedom in that boat. Heber later joined the IRC staff and was largely responsible for the remarkable success of the IRC children's home in Hainbach, Austria.

helped one refugee after another cross to safety. Suddenly a woman with a swollen belly ran toward the border and stumbled to the ground. Minutes passed, no one moved. Shots were heard. At last a volunteer rushed to the woman who had fallen. Once she was revived, the group learned that she was eight months pregnant. All of her life was compressed into one basic instinct, unmistakable in this moment: her child had to be born in freedom.

The burden of so many refugees was more than Austria could cope with. The International Rescue Committee stepped up its activities in several European countries. IRC's Paris office focused on occupational rehabilitation. Health and training centers

ABOVE:

Hungarian refugees who were given asylum in Belgium were helped by IRC.

RIGHT:

IRC also assisted Hungarians who made their way to Yugoslavia.

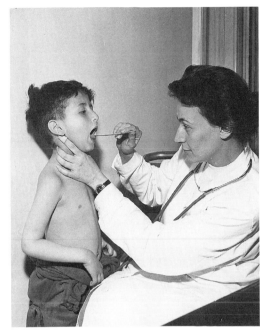

TOP, LEFT:

Paul Heber, an American of Hungarian origin, rushed to Austria in November 1956 to help IRC develop programs for uprooted children.

TOP, RIGHT AND BOTTOM:

Medical and educational services were provided by IRC for thousands of Hungarian refugee children in western Europe.

IRC vice president Claiborne Pell (now an IRC board member and chairman of the U.S. Senate Foreign Relations Committee) went to Austria to help organize refugee programs. Among the projects was a mobile library with fifteen hundred Hungarian books that toured the refugee camps.

were established in Great Britain, Belgium, West Germany, and Sweden. Special attention was directed toward orphans, unaccompanied children, and adolescents. A children's home in Switzerland received many Hungarians.

IRC worked at combating the effects of idleness, a scourge for refugees. Small libraries were opened where refugees congregated, and later a mobile library was added. A symphony of refugee musicians, the Hungaria Philharmonica, was organized. A Hungarian handicraft shop was opened, and young refugees were enrolled in trade schools.

IRC brought several leaders of the revolution to the United States to tell their stories to the American people and to policy makers. Among them was Joseph Kovago, mayor of Budapest, who had been a key figure in Hungary's anti-Nazi movement, barely escaping execution by the Gestapo. From 1950 to 1956 he had been imprisoned by the Communists. When released he had been elected president of the revolutionary National Committee of Budapest as well as mayor of that city.

Paul Jonas also came to the United States under the sponsorship of IRC. Jonas was president of the Petofi Circle, the group that helped spark the revolt in Hungary. He too

Monsignor Bela Varga joined Leo Cherne and IRC in 1956 to support the cause of a free Hungary, and then the refugees. He had served as a leader in the anti-Nazi underground movement in Hungary during the 1930s and was responsible for the escape of thousands of Hungarian Jews as well as Poles. He was a member of the Hungarian parliament and, at the time of the Communist take-over in 1948, was president. Again he went underground until, faced with imminent capture by Soviet forces, he escaped to the United States. In 1990, when Hungary became a free country, he was invited to return to his homeland, and he turned over presidency of the parliament to the new democratically elected government. Monsignor Varga has been a member of the board of directors of IRC for the past thirty-five years.

▶ ▶ ▶ ▶

RIGHT:

Many American organizations, such as Meals for Millions, provided food and relief supplies to IRC for distribution in European refugee camps for Hungarians.

BELOW:

Hungaria Philharmonica, an orchestra composed of refugee musicians, was organized with the help of IRC.

had spent years in prison because of his outspoken anti-Nazi and anti-Communist views. Once in America, he resumed his scholarly career in economics. Like thousands of refugees, however, Jonas never recovered from his forced flight. Although extremely grateful for the generosity of America, he had paid a heavy price for freedom: he had had to leave his homeland. Twenty years after his arrival in the Unites States he penned an article for *Harper's* magazine in which he eloquently expressed his intense nostalgia for home—something that had never diminished—and his deep sense of loss.

In the United States IRC's heavy Hungarian resettlement caseload included students and teachers, scientists and engineers, writers and artists, physicians and lawyers. Language was a serious barrier, prompting IRC to open a language center in New York City that at its peak served almost a thousand refugees. A similar center was established in Canada.

Eventually Hungary passed out of the headlines, but the problems for refugees did not fade away. IRC continued to serve those in need. Long after the revolution had been crushed IRC was working to relocate refugees and integrate them into new environments.

The impact of the revolution did not fade away either. The Western world had united around the freedom fighters. The entire political and social spectrum was there, ready to help.

"It was an extraordinary moment," Angier Duke remembers. "There was no reluctance on the part of any free people to respond. We simply did what had to be done." Duke continues: "Hungary escalated IRC into a world-class organization. We were at the vanguard of a worldwide effort. IRC, like the world, was changed."

Refugee assistance had been recast. Once it had been the preoccupation of a handful, but now refugees were becoming the concern of many. Something new was being brought to the attention of Americans and free people everywhere.

IRC sponsored English-language schools for Hungarian refugees admitted to the United States and Canada.

The world had come together on the bridge at Andau. And the International Rescue Committee had emerged a leader, impassioned and ready to protect any who seek freedom.

Eleanor Roosevelt joined Leo Cherne in asking the American people to support the cause of Hungarians now in exile.

Refugee Assistance Expands

▶ ▶ ▶ ▶ ▶ ▶ ▶ ▶ ▶ ▶

By the late 1950s, a quarter century after it was founded, the International Rescue Committee was no longer an agency assisting only European refugees. Refugee crises around the world required responses. IRC, by necessity, was becoming global.

IRC was assisting Jewish refugees fleeing religious oppression in Algeria, Morocco, Tunisia, and Egypt; defecting African and Asian students; Indonesians who came to the United States once the Dutch left their country; and Cubans who fled when Castro came to power in 1959. By the early 1960s Haitians and Chinese would be added to the list of those being assisted.

Around the world large numbers of people were moving away from tyranny and toward freedom. Albanians, Bulgarians, and Yugoslavs were migrating to Greece. Sweden had become a country of first asylum for Poles escaping across the Baltic Sea. Thousands who refused to be suppressed by the Soviet Union fled Czechoslovakia, Hungary, Poland, and Romania.

Clinics addressing both physical and psychological needs were established in Austria, West Germany, Belgium, Italy, and Spain. IRC cooperated with the United Nations High Commissioner for Refugees and other voluntary agencies throughout Europe. Financial support came from private sources in the United States as well as overseas sources such as the Norwegian Refugee Council and West German trade unions. Responding to refugee crises was becoming an international effort.

There was no predicting what new oppression might send the next stream of refugees into exile. To prepare for the challenges ahead, IRC established a commission to examine the issues confronting refugees, explore ways of responding to emergencies that uproot large numbers of people, and raise the awareness of citizens around the world. The commission was chaired by IRC president Angier Duke and Harold I. Zellerbach, president of the Crown-Zellerbach Corporation. Members included diplomats, representatives of trade unions, leaders of religious bodies, and foreign affairs experts.

The commission determined that IRC's initial tasks were to heal the wounds of the thousands of people displaced by World War II and to prepare the international community for the reality that refugee assistance was becoming a permanent responsibility of the free world.

New receiving centers and camps were established in Western Europe during the 1950s as refugees continued to flee from behind the Iron Curtain.

A group of refugees left behind watch the departure of friends who have been granted asylum in the United States.

As IRC was expanding its efforts, the United Nations too was recognizing the seriousness of the refugee issue. Its General Assembly adopted a resolution designating the year beginning June 1959 as World Refugee Year.

The International Rescue Committee led the way as the free world committed itself to serving refugees wherever and whenever they were forced to flee political unrest or civil strife, religious or racial persecution, or any threat to freedom.

The Long Saga of Indochinese Refugees

▶ ▶ ▶ ▶ ▶ ▶ ▶ ▶ ▶ ▶

In 1954, following the defeat of the French colonial forces and the division of their country, nearly one million North Vietnamese fled to South Vietnam. Not the least of the problems faced by the new Saigon government was the influx of refugees from Communist-ruled North Vietnam. IRC chairman Leo Cherne was soon in Saigon to review the situation and to initiate an assistance program for the refugees.

Following Cherne's report and recommendations, the IRC board of directors dispatched its vice chairman, Joseph Buttinger, to South Vietnam. He immediately recognized the refugees' extraordinary desire for freedom and the tremendous reservoir of talent, skills, and professional expertise within the refugee community.

Buttinger was a wise choice to establish IRC's program in Vietnam. He had been a leader in the anti-Nazi underground in his native Austria during the 1930s. His experience as a refugee, first in France and then in the United States, provided him with insight that proved valuable in Vietnam.

IRC's program, designed in consultation with South Vietnam's new premier, Ngo Dinh Diem, sought not only to relieve mass suffering but also to take advantage of the resources available within the refugee community. It included direct aid to refugees and a network of education programs designed to develop skills that would benefit the entire country.

Financial and technical assistance was offered to indigenous groups such as the Popular Cultural Association, a private nonprofit educational organization of Vietnamese refugees who had studied abroad. This group sponsored the Popular Technical Institute, which offered evening classes in languages and social sciences. The institute conducted classes in towns all over South Vietnam. It is estimated that the Popular Cultural Association taught more than a hundred thousand Vietnamese to read and write.

IRC soon joined with other voluntary agencies to launch Operation Brotherhood, an effort to deliver medical aid and public sanitation to hundreds of thousands of refugees in rural villages. The project was successful, preventing much-feared epidemics. All these activities had a profound psychological impact on the people, by demonstrating that the world was genuinely concerned about the plight of this small, war-ravaged country.

While IRC worked in South Vietnam in the mid-1950s, the West was struggling with the Hungarian revolution and its aftermath. From Vietnam came an inspiring response. The Vietnamese collected $70,000 that was forwarded to IRC to help Hungarian refugees.

After the Geneva agreement of 1954 partitioning Vietnam, one million people from the north fled to the new independent country of South Vietnam.

Leo Cherne flew to Saigon immediately after the partitioning. He was followed by IRC vice chairman Joseph A. Buttinger (center), who put into motion a network of programs for the vast refugee population. Buttinger had been a leader of the Austrian anti-Nazi underground during the 1930s.

Identification tags were pinned on Vietnamese refugee children in case they were separated from their parents while in flight. IRC's early work in South Vietnam included schooling for displaced boys and girls.

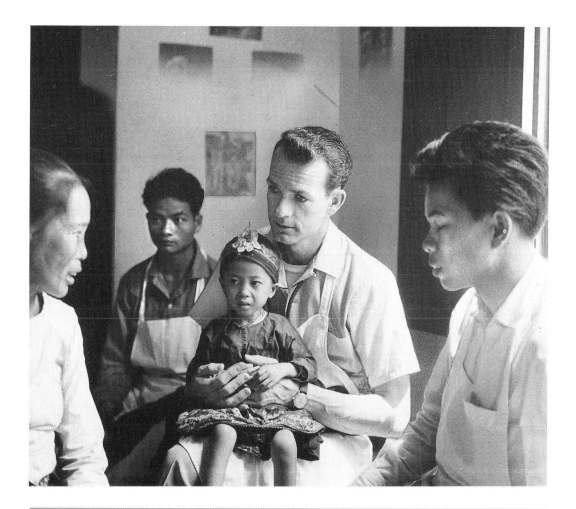

IRC's work in Vietnam yielded an important side effect. A young American doctor named Tom Dooley had been working with refugees in North Vietnam in 1951. Upon his discharge from the Navy he decided that he wanted to continue serving refugees. He went to Laos, where for two years he ran a clinic under the auspices of IRC. His work was not unlike that of Dr. Albert Schweitzer in French equatorial Africa and Dr. Gordon Seagrave in Burma.

The experiences of these three doctors led to the idea of creating an international medical service to bring modern medicine to remote regions of the world. IRC chairman Leo Cherne met with Dr. Schweitzer, and MEDICO (Medical International Cooperation) was born. Dr. Schweitzer endorsed the idea "with all my heart." Today MEDICO is an integrated service of CARE, the international relief cooperative that IRC helped found.

▶ ▶ ▶ ▶

ABOVE:

A makeshift bunker of sand-bags becomes a temporary home for this Vietnamese orphan.

RIGHT AND OPPOSITE:

A network of child care centers provided nutritious meals, recreation, and educational services for displaced Vietnamese boys and girls.

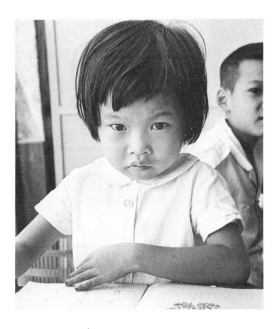

By 1960 the primary task of resettling and assimilating the refugees from North Vietnam had been completed. Emergency programs were phased out and long-term projects were handed over to indigenous groups. That same year IRC left South Vietnam, not knowing that within four years it would be back.

In 1964, as violence in Vietnam escalated, IRC returned to help the growing number of refugees, especially the children. By 1965 more refugees were on the move than had been during the initial exodus from North Vietnam in 1954. IRC workers went into action, focusing on strengthening existing institutions.

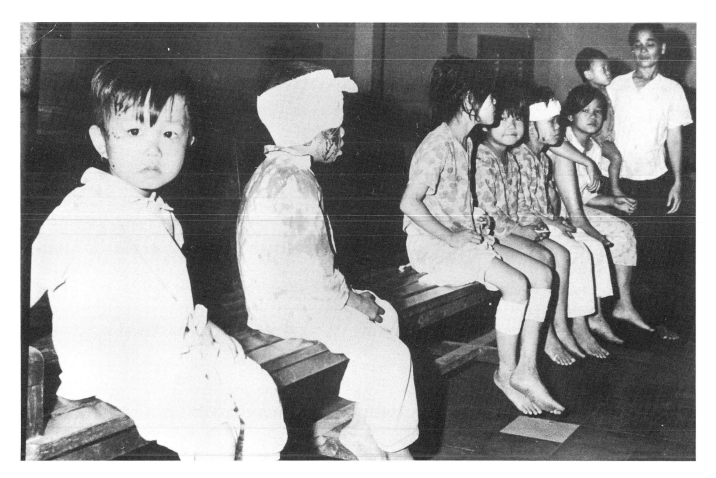

The number of sick and wounded Vietnamese civilians multiplied as the war spread, and IRC established medical facilities for the children in particular. One of IRC's volunteer physicians was Dr. Ernst Fenelon (right), a Haitian refugee, who worked at a dispensary in Quang Ngai Province.

IRC's 120-bed reception and convalescent center in Saigon served the plastic and reconstructive surgery hospital operated by Children's Medical Relief International.

IRC expanded a network of day care centers, allowing parents to work, and monitored the medical and nutritional health of the children at these centers. Classrooms for refugee children were funded and provided with supplies. Nurses were sent into orphanages. These and other children's facilities eventually became self-sufficient by operating small farming and other income-generating projects.

Medical and public health facilities were opened and staffed by volunteer doctors, nurses, and paramedics. In Saigon IRC's 120-bed reception and convalescent center augmented Vietnam's leading facility for reconstructive surgery, providing twenty-four-hour pre- and postoperative care to children undergoing surgery.

Health conditions in South Vietnam were desperate. It was estimated that there were no more than a thousand physicians in the country, 60 percent of whom were serving with the armed forces. Physicians willing to commit at least eighteen months of service were recruited. IRC rushed teams of doctors to the scene, where they were confronted with frustration and disappointment. A letter from a doctor at one of IRC's outposts described the situation:

I want to tell you about this morning in Tung Uyen. When we arrived there were no patients. But fifteen minutes later more than two hundred surrounded us, showing in their faces their illnesses as well as their desire to be cured. A sick mother with a dying child in her arms and three other feverish children hanging on to her skirt impressed me most. I could do nothing for the dying child. I did not have the proper medicine. We worked in a small room, three feet square. We almost suffocated, and through the window and door all we could see were the anxious faces of sick people. But we had neither enough nor the right medicines, and this is the greatest difficulty a doctor in Vietnam has to cope with.

Although America's pharmaceutical industry responded generously, there was never enough, nor was there always available the right medicine at the right place and time. Despite these difficulties, doctors not only met their commitments of eighteen months, but many volunteered to remain for a second or even third tour of duty.

A special health care program was initiated to meet the needs of the Montagnards. These hilltribe people were held in contempt by other Vietnamese, and they rarely received the benefit of whatever medical care was available. IRC-trained health workers provided services and care to these people of the central highlands.

It was clear that the problems of the refugees were not temporary. A program of economic development and integration was essential. Handicraft schools were opened, materials and tools were supplied, and agriculture projects were started. Income generation and self-sufficiency were stressed. Rural development teams were extremely effective in providing assistance and boosting the morale of

people forced into idleness for far too long. The refugees wanted nothing more than to be able to take care of themselves and their families.

Typical was the group assembled by IRC at Ap Doi Mon (New Life Hamlet), where a village for six thousand war refugees was constructed. First a dispensary opened and medical supplies were obtained, then a sanitation plan was put into place. Next gardens were plotted adjacent to each dwelling. In keeping with local custom, a fish pond was dug and stocked, providing for a steady

supply of protein. A chicken-breeding project began. Soon a school opened and a community center was completed. Human dignity refused to be dampened by the horrors of war.

In this as in any refugee situation, it was IRC's desire that its presence become unnecessary. Once a self-sustaining community was established, IRC withdrew. IRC's supervisor at Ap Doi Mon reported the following:

> How much progress has been made can be judged by the fact that the time has come for the IRC team to phase out its activities here. The village is now basically capable of maintaining itself. There is a functioning school, a community center, and a medical dispensary in what two years ago was nothing but a barren plot of land. The chicken project and fish pond are now run by cooperatives of hamlet residents, housing has been improved, and local elections have been held. One project will be maintained for some time to come—a training class in carpentry, a much-needed skill in the area. The initiator, organizer, and teacher of this course is a young Navy Seabee who became so committed to helping the refugees that he returned as a civilian to work with them.

The success of this project led to the setting up of similar village reconstruction projects in several locations.

Following the cease-fire and withdrawal of American troops in April 1973, it was evident that the plight of refugees would only worsen. IRC sent a fact-finding mission of board members to tour the country and consult with hundreds of concerned people. The agency committed itself to remaining and increasing its services, especially those for children.

The mission's report led to the establishment in Saigon of a seventy-bed rehabilitative center for war orphans, which enabled some children to become candidates for adoption. In its first year of operation the center treated four thousand orphans, a thousand of whom were placed in permanent homes abroad. The

In April 1973, immediately after an agreement for a cease-fire was reached, an IRC fact-finding mission flew to Saigon to investigate evolving refugee problems during this comparative time of peace. The delegation, which visited a score of refugee areas throughout South Vietnam, included (left to right) Alton Kastner, IRC deputy director, and IRC board members Cecil Lyon, David Sher, Isadore Scott, rapporteur Robin Chandler Duke, Angier Duke (mission leader), and Anthony D. Duke. A principal recommendation of the mission, adopted by the board of directors, was to develop a rehabilitation program for Vietnamese orphans to qualify them for overseas adoption.

FLIGHT

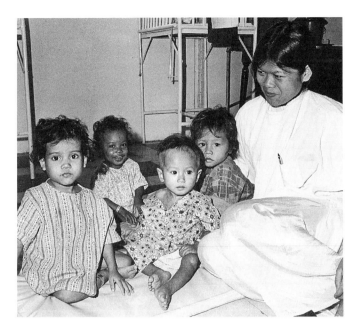

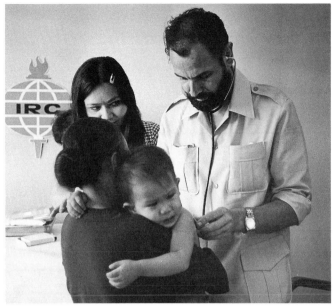

By December 1975 a single IRC rehabilitation hospital in Saigon had admitted four thousand war orphans. More than eight hundred of the children were subsequently placed with adoptive parents overseas—primarily in the United States—through adoption agencies operating in Vietnam.

A few of the Vietnamese orphans arrive in the United States to be met by their new parents.

On April 30, 1975, Hanoi's military forces occupied Saigon, all but completing their conquest of South Vietnam, in violation of the cease-fire agreement. This little girl and her baby brother were among the multitude of civilians trying to escape the Communist take-over and seeking safe haven in whatever country they might reach.

When Hanoi's forces rolled into Saigon on April 30, 1975, IRC's work in South Vietnam—work that had begun twenty-one years earlier—came to an end. The Vietcong victory forced a massive flight of tens of thousands of Indochinese refugees. Would-be escapees climbed the walls of the American embassy in Saigon and pleaded for help. Over a hundred thousand succeeded in reaching American ships off the coast. During a ten-week period 135,000 Vietnamese were processed for resettlement in the United States.

The first of the Vietnamese refugees resettled by IRC settled in Hartford, Connecticut, under the sponsorship of a community group called Stepping Stones. This group had been organized by a Hungarian refugee who had been resettled by IRC in 1957. Soon the Cuban refugee community in Miami hosted an IRC-sponsored group of thirty-one Vietnamese. Cuban volunteers in New Orleans followed this example by welcoming refugees. This practice of refugees helping refugees became a mainstay of IRC's resettlement efforts all around the country. It continues today.

As more and more Vietnamese arrived in the United States, IRC set up processing operations at the four military bases that had become refugee camps. Soon thirty full-time resettlement workers were in these camps, joined by scores of volunteers. Among the staff was Robert P. DeVecchi, who ten years later became IRC's executive director and in 1992 was named its president.

The need to assimilate so many people so quickly put a strain on an already weak economy, but the feeling of most Americans was clear: those forced out of Vietnam were welcome and deserving of refuge.

Government relocation centers were opened in California, Arkansas, Florida, and Pennsylvania. Top priority was given to finding sponsors, who would help the

success of this center resulted in others being opened in Da Nang and Qui Nhon. A women's training project in home day care was expanded in Saigon, leading to a network of sixty-three centers caring for hundreds of children.

IRC continued to provide services for the Montagnards. With the help of the An Quang Buddhists, IRC constructed a simple wood-frame, metal-roof day care center that received 115 Montagnard children.

Welcome to Houston

During a ten-week period following the exodus from Vietnam, close to 135,000 refugees entered the United States, joined by 5,000 Cambodians escaping the Khmer Rouge. This massive emigration, occurring without preparation by either the refugees or their host country, led to the most intensive resettlement effort conducted by IRC since its founding. New resettlement offices were soon opened by IRC in response to the massive influx.

FLIGHT

ABOVE:

Refugees from Laos, too, were escaping the Communist conquest of their country, including this group waving good-bye to loved ones in a Thailand camp, en route to Bangkok and then the United States.

RIGHT:

Some Vietnamese fled by boat to Malaysia, where this family of six, granted asylum in the United States, awaits a plane to freedom.

In February 1976, the year after Vietnam, Cambodia, and Laos fell to Communist forces, refugees fled by land and sea to other Southeast Asian nations. Among those seeking safety were Vietnamese boat people.

refugees in finding jobs and in beginning the process of integrating into a new life and culture. By December 1975 the government-sponsored reception centers were closed.

By this time IRC had opened sixteen regional resettlement offices around the country. All told, IRC helped several thousand Vietnamese refugees begin new lives in the United States during these hectic months in 1975.

The new regime in Vietnam failed to change the conditions that forced people to seek freedom. Refugees continued to flow out of the country, to escape the "re-education"

camps or being sent into servitude in the jungle, the country's "new economic zones." The phenomenon of the Vietnamese boat people began.

The mass movement out of Vietnam was both escape and expulsion. The government used the cover of the exodus of refugees to conceal its forcing out of undesirables. Exiles sought refuge on whatever seafaring vessel would carry them away.

The laws of the sea were abandoned. Leaky boats in distress, overcrowded with refugees, were not offered the assistance that had always been the law of the sea. Captains and crews

In November 1979 the Pulitzer Prize–winning journalist Henry Kamm wrote:

Seventeen Vietnamese refugees, including four young children, were murdered by Thai fishermen at sea and most of the thirty-seven women aboard four refugee boats were raped many times by about five hundred fishermen during a period of twenty-two days.

Local police acknowledged that fifty-seven boats had visited the scene reported on by Kamm to participate in the rapes and beatings. A pilot flying over spotted bodies floating in the water while fishing boats stood by. Representatives of the United High Commissioner for Refugees who came to help were threatened with violence.

During the war in Southeast Asia, Laos, too had become a battlefield. In 1975 the Pathet Lao triumphed and an oppressive Communist regime came to power in Vientiane. Another exodus began as thousands of

watched as thousands of men, women, and children drowned. Lawless pirates added to the tragic toll, killing refugees, kidnapping and raping women and girls, and sinking boats.

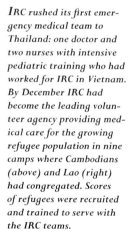

IRC rushed its first emergency medical team to Thailand: one doctor and two nurses with intensive pediatric training who had worked for IRC in Vietnam. By December IRC had become the leading volunteer agency providing medical care for the growing refugee population in nine camps where Cambodians (above) and Lao (right) had congregated. Scores of refugees were recruited and trained to serve with the IRC teams.

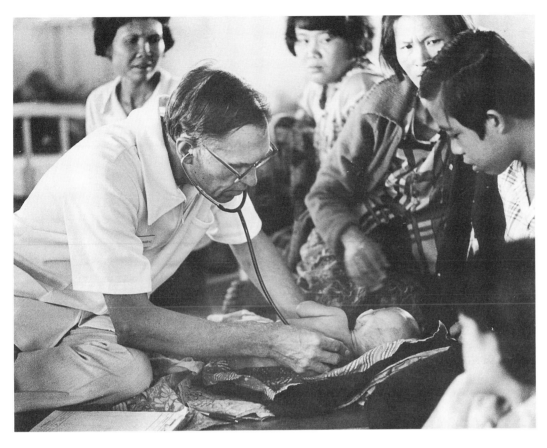

As the refugee flow to Thailand expanded, IRC intensified its work for the Indochinese children. This pediatrician from Kentucky, Dr. Kenneth Rasmussen, was among the scores of IRC medical volunteers.

lowland and highland Lao refugees fled across the Mekong River into Thailand.

Among them were the Hmong, or "free people" as they called themselves. The Hmong had once lived quiet lives rooted in a simple subsistence economy in the mountains of Laos. But they were soon pressed into service by the United States and for many years bore the brunt of the secret war in Laos. Not unlike the Montagnards of Vietnam, they were considered enemies by most everyone. The Hmong quickly became a target of harsh persecution.

The majority lowland Lao, too, resented the hegemony of Hanoi. As the oppressive regime tightened its grasp on Laos, flight across the Mekong River accelerated.

In Cambodia the overthrow of the Lon Nol government gave way to the genocidal atrocities of the Khmer Rouge. In 1979 Vietnam invaded that country. This drove out

the Khmer Rouge but also caused hundreds of thousands to flee to the border of Thailand. Thailand had become the destination of not only Cambodians but of Lao and Vietnamese as well. Sick, starving, and wounded, these refugees were in desperate need.

IRC had by now become the leading voluntary agency serving Indochinese refugees, with teams of doctors, nurses, paramedics, public health experts, teachers, child care specialists, and sanitarians in more than fourteen refugee camps.

Medical and nutritional services were a first priority. Hospitals that included pediatric wards, pharmacies, and laboratories were established. Milk-distribution sheds soon attracted long lines of children. Maternal and child care was offered, as well as counseling about family planning. IRC medics visited detention centers where "illegal immigrants" were held. Malnutrition

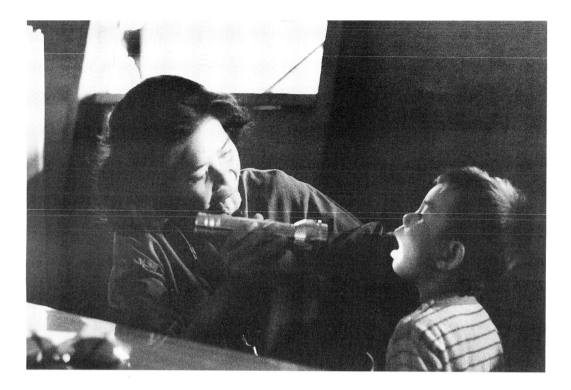

and the brain damage that often results from severe malnutrition were serious problems among the refugees.

One of IRC's leading doctors in Thailand was Dr. Dominica P. Garcia, a physician from the Philippines. Her sensitivity was demonstrated in her medical care as well as in her eloquent summaries of the work being done with the refugees:

> Reports from Hmong newcomers are truly distressing. With their little crops destroyed by poison gas, they leave their villages with no food provisions. For weeks they hide in mountain jungles avoiding Vietnamese and Pathet Lao patrols. They eat roots and leaves, sometimes poisonous mushrooms. Nobody dares beg for rice from Lao settlements. Many contract malaria; whiplashes from brambles and bushes get infected and become festering ulcers; their feet are terribly swollen. When enemy troops sight them, they are fired upon and a number sustain gunshot wounds which, too, get readily infected.
>
> Out of the thousands who leave the villages only a few hundred reach the river, where more are decimated by drowning. Women with babies strapped to their backs are so faint with hunger, pain, and fear that they lose consciousness while being towed by the "stronger" members of the family. When they regain consciousness, the babies at their backs have died by drowning.
>
> The Mekong River at this time is quite swollen and debris swirls wildly in the current. Being mountain people, the Hmongs are helpless in water and cannot swim. They grab on to any number of floating objects, banana stalks, dead limbs of trees. A few manage to bring empty plastic gallon containers, still others inflate ordinary grocery plastic bags. It is not unusual to find these survivors clinging to their makeshift "life-savers" even long after they have been in the detention centers. They carry them up to the hospital wards where they finally get proper treatment.
>
> The horror and misery of their flight to safety is etched in their blank, tear-stained faces. Men and women weep readily at the nightmarish memory of their ordeal. Husbands, wives, children, parents have been lost in the process. Gone is the familiar look of ini-

tial elation found among newcomers. One is ready to assume that they know very little the difference between communism and freedom. Their main concern is to escape oppression and annihilation of their tribes.

The IRC medical team is almost always on the spot to render first aid to the new arrivals. No one knows for sure when they come, but the need to follow up treatment and change wound dressings of previous cases almost daily prepares the team for any new ones coming. Antibiotics, vitamins, fever pills are literally dropped into the mouths of semiconscious patients. Abscesses are incised, drained, and dressed, ulcers debrided, gunshot wounds cleaned and stitched, recent abrasions painted with disinfectant. Bandage, gauze, cotton, and plaster are used by the kilograms. Cleaning salves and tinctures flow. They deserve every little help we can give them.

Evidence of the horrors taking place in Cambodia under the Khmer Rouge emerged gradually. The world was reluctant to accept the reality.

Losses in Cambodia were staggering. The genocide was cruelly calculating. First targets were intellectuals, teachers, and doctors. The plan to eradicate a culture continued with the plundering of the schools.

Some citizens of the world refused to be silent. Leo Cherne was one of them. He invited public debates with apologists for the new regimes in Indochina and fired off letter after letter to agencies and advocates of human rights.

Another who refused to look away was Sydney Schanberg of the *New York Times*. He persisted in calling attention to the atrocities. As early as 1975 he had witnessed the mass deportation of a million people from the city of Phnom Penh. He watched as men, women, and children were marched through the streets, having had only minutes to prepare for whatever was ahead. He told of the lack of food, water, and medicine, and of

families pushing hospital beds along rutted roads—scenes repeated in city after city. Above all he persevered in the search for his friend and translator, Dith Pran. IRC participated in this effort and eventually helped them reunite. Dith Pran now serves on the IRC board.

By early 1980 IRC staff in Thailand numbered 105 doctors, nurses, and paramedics supported by an even larger number of refugees being trained on the job. Among the most creative and innovative programs was a collaboration with the New York Hospital–Cornell Medical Center that provided "release time" to personnel willing to serve in Thailand. Volunteer doctors, residents, and nurses, working for two to six months, staffed hospitals and trained refugees in first aid and medical support services. The founder of this program, Dr. Theodore Li, now serves on the IRC board.

At Khao-I-Dang, the Cambodian refugee camp in Thailand, the population soared to over 120,000. It was the largest concentration of Cambodians in the world in 1980. IRC developed a constellation of programs, providing refugees with critical care as well as a multitude of skills needed to face the future. Expatriate staff and volunteers, Thai nationals, and refugee professionals offered assistance and training.

The following letter from Khao-I-Dang was typical of reports received.

The cases come every day. Most get better but too many die. For those who get well, there is a great joy around, playing and joking and happy scenes of departure when they leave. You hope it will be those that will stay in your memory, but it is the ones that break your heart that stay the most vivid. Like the grandfather who buried all but one of his children and grandchildren in Cambodia, and brought in his last sick grandson. A day later, the little

child just faded away. Then a teenage girl carried in her little brother stricken with meningitis. As we tried to save him through the night, she stood close by, touching him, sponging him off and weeping. When he died, she quietly left, leaving her brother on the floor wrapped in an old blanket.

With just a few tattered school books smuggled across the border, IRC was able to reproduce texts, write new ones, and build a foundation for a primary and secondary school system that at its peak served over fifty thousand refugee children and young adults. Thousands of refugees were trained to serve as teachers.

IRC's ingenuity was particularly evident in its schools for disabled refugees. Many Cambodian children, handicapped at birth or by torture or exploding mines, were, at first, left at home while their siblings went to school. Thanks to IRC, disabled children were able to attend school. Sign language and

ABOVE:

Providing clean water and sanitation systems were high among the priorities of IRC's refugee work.

RIGHT:

This tent city was among the many new camps that proliferated throughout Thailand as the flight of Indochinese refugees continued unabated.

Braille systems for Cambodian children were developed. They had never before existed, and now handicapped children were able to join other children in school.

The human tragedy in Cambodia was further complicated in the early 1980s by famine. The granaries in Cambodia were empty and no seed was available for planting. This catastrophe added to the numbers and needs of Cambodian refugees. IRC quickly dispatched more medical teams to the camps along the Thailand-Cambodia border.

Processing as many refugees as possible for permanent resettlement elsewhere became a high priority. IRC provided the staff to facilitate the processing of refugees for resettlement in the United States. Some seventy staff members based in Bangkok moved into the camps for weeks at a time, to help refugees register and qualify for resettlement in the United States and other countries offering asylum.

In the United States, where thousands of Vietnamese and Lao as well as Cambodians were resettled, IRC's regional offices played a

A lone Cambodian girl awaits a doctor's visit at an IRC clinic.

significant role. Caseworkers found housing and jobs for the refugees, provided education and skills training, and helped refugees integrate into the social, cultural, and economic life of a new environment.

Dang Nguyen, the head of one refugee family now in America, was quoted in the *New York Times:* "I have a steady job, regular raises, a nice place to live, the children work hard, help out, get all *A*s, my wife and I are well, we have grandchildren, and next month there will be a big event in our family: we will all get our citizenship papers!"

In an effort to awaken public awareness to the magnitude of the Indochinese refugee problem and to effect policy, Leo Cherne organized, in 1977, the Citizens Commission on Indochinese Refugees. The commission comprised a cross-section of America's political, cultural, and religious leaders, including James Michener, Bayard Rustin, Rabbi Marc Tanenbaum, and others.

Commission members visited refugee camps and met with government officials in Southeast Asia. Their visits proved effective. The Thai government saw the coming of the commission as a sign that Thailand would not be left alone to carry the burden of the tens of thousands of refugees. Back home the commission found a receptive audience for its recommendations. Many fact-finding missions were conducted by the commission over several years as part of an advocacy effort that had a significant impact on the lives of Indochinese refugees.

On April 26, 1978, the *Wall Street Journal* published an editorial that included the following passage:

> *This past February, the International Rescue Committee, which has long been aiding refugees around the world for some 45 years,*

Commission members Rabbi Marc Tanenbaum and William J. Casey with Vietnamese refugee children in Hong Kong.

On an island off the Malaysian coast, Vietnamese boat people wait to greet a Citizens Commission delegation.

sent a study commission of prominent Americans to take a first-hand look at the refugees' situation in Asia. The visitors found what they had expected: that the problem was big enough to demand further U.S. action. . . .

Their effort succeeded. At the end of March, the AFL-CIO's executive council issued a statement not only voicing no objection to more refugee admissions but actively supporting the idea. And a statement signed by 90 of the country's most prominent black leaders called on President Carter to act. Unemployment was certainly a problem, they thought; but "we oppose the dehumanizing tendency of placing price tags on the heads of Indochinese refugees." These positions seem to have played a significant part in finally forming the administration policy.

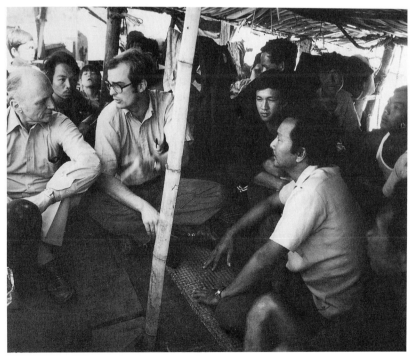

From the late 1970s on, IRC developed a far-ranging network of humanitarian services for Indochinese refugees crowding the camps of Southeast Asia. The work consisted largely of medical, sanitation, education, child care, resettlement, training, and self-help programs. The recommendations of the Citizens Commission on Indochinese Refugees served as a catalyst for the expansion of services.

▶ ▶ ▶ ▶

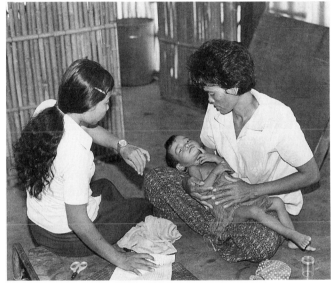

In Thailand alone, IRC medical facilities were staffed by hundreds of expatriate doctors, nurses, and paramedics in addition to refugees recruited and trained by the American personnel.

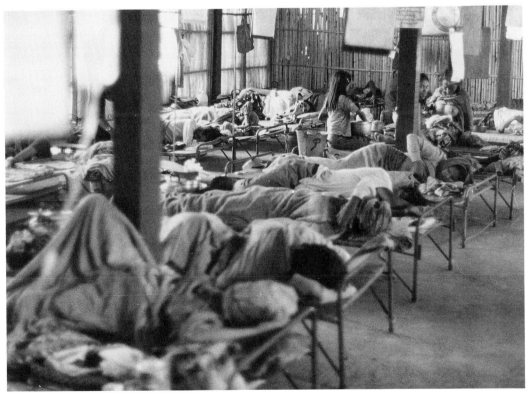

Dr. Daniel L. Weiner, a board member now serving as chair of IRC's medical committee, went to Thailand to evaluate the programs.

By 1981 an IRC school system in Thailand exclusively for Cambodian refugees was serving close to forty thousand children in primary and secondary schools.

On Pulau Bidong Island off Malaysia, where thirty thousand Vietnamese boat people lived on the edge of disaster, an IRC public health program included latrines for the refugees.

IRC programs in industrial arts and farming enabled Indochinese refugees in Thailand to become self-supporting.

On the Thailand side of the Poipet Bridge, Leo Cherne, leader of the 1980 March for Survival, pleaded with border officials to allow the food and medical convoy to enter Cambodia. His plea was denied and the supplies were given to needy Cambodian refugees in Thailand.

By early 1980 public attention toward the plight of Cambodians was waning. IRC recognized the need to restore the Cambodian crisis to the top of the world's humanitarian agenda and searched for a dramatic way to call attention to the plight of the refugees. IRC joined forces with Medecins sans Frontieres in organizing "Cambodia: March for Suvival."

This plan called for a convoy of trucks in Thailand, laden with food and medicines, to make its way toward Cambodia. Once at the border, relief workers and prominent citizens from around the world accompanying the convoy would plead for entry into Cambodia. If permission was denied, as was feared, all the supplies would then be turned over to Cambodian refugees along the border.

Elie Wiesel agreed to join in this effort, as did the Russian dissident Alexander Ginzburg and the British parliamentarian Winston Churchill III. Among those who played a significant role in rallying support was Joan Baez, who had long been promoting pacifist resistance to American policy in Indochina. She called upon her friends and colleagues to join her as she journeyed to Southeast Asia.

One of the most important participants in the march was Liv Ullmann, who had this to say to a gathering of journalists:

Haven't there been other marches for freedom where the marchers were asked to be silent because things would eventually be worked out if one at the moment were only a little careful and diplomatic? Thank you, Martin Luther King, for not listening to those warnings. Has there not been a smell from the pipes of certain ovens in Poland that some people wondered about, and did not those who "knew" and even inspected the camps of these ovens, for some diplomatic reason, keep quiet about them? Was not our great excuse, when we finally found out,

Among the many prominent human rights activists who participated in the March for Survival were Liv Ull- mann, Bayard Rustin, and IRC staff member John Crowley.

that we did not know, we did not see? I will be quiet no more. I want to do this march. I want to go to the border and see myself if it is really true that they will not let us in with food and medicine. I want to go that road tomorrow because it is the same road as the road to the gas chambers; and I will not be the one later to say I did not know, I did not see, I did not hear.

This group of citizens from the world over, armed only with food and medicines, arrived on a dusty road at Aranyaprathet and the Poipet Bridge only to be turned away.

Leo Cherne took a bullhorn into his hands and pleaded with the border guard. But the soldiers threatened to do what they had already announced they would—fire if Cherne took another step toward Cambodia.

The group gathered along the border sat down in the dust for five solemn minutes of silence.

The marchers did go home having failed to cross the border. The relief supplies were delivered to refugees within Thailand. Despite a cynical press, the event had captured the world's attention. Clearly the Cambodians were not forgotten. This small group of con-

cerned citizens of the world proved that a small band of people can arrest attention, influence attitudes, and affect policy. Communities around the world opened themselves as host communities for refugees desiring to resettle. Countries of first asylum agreed to keep their borders open to Cambodians seeking refuge, despite internal pressures to close their doors.

IRC remained committed to the thousands of Cambodians who remained in Thailand, unable to qualify for admission into the United States or other countries of asylum. An important part of IRC's efforts was a cultural program of music and dance, fine arts and crafts, and theatre, intended to restore the cultural heritage that had been wiped out by the Khmer Rouge. IRC also opened a print shop where Cambodian books and school texts were produced.

ABOVE:

Joan Baez at the March for Survival.

LEFT:

Alexander Ginzburg, the Russian dissident, and Elie Wiesel, an IRC board member, also joined the march.

A tracing program was established to determine whether unaccompanied children were indeed orphans or whether they had been separated from their parents during flight. Through this program over two thousand presumed orphans were reunited with their families.

In March 1982 the Citizens Commission on Indochinese Refugees dispatched civil rights leader Bayard Rustin and civic leader Catherine O'Neill to Thailand to investigate two developments: the piracy taking place in the Gulf of Thailand and the ban on Cambo-

Thousands of Cambodian children arrived alone in Thailand, where IRC initiated an elaborate tracing program to determine if they were indeed orphans or whether they might have surviving family members. The work produced dramatic results: more than two thousand children were reunited with parents or other family members, some of them in distant countries.

In order to preserve the Cambodian culture that had been destroyed by the Khmer Rouge, IRC developed programs for the refugees focusing on dance, music, art, and literature.

dian refugee admissions to the United States. The commission substantiated the brutality and abduction of refugees. Upon returning, members testified before legislative leaders as well as representatives of the executive branch. An appeal was made for an antipiracy program, and for the admission of Cambodian refugees into the United States.

IRC delivered humanitarian assistance to Indochinese refugees not only in Thailand but also in Hong Kong and Malaysia. Public health, sanitation, and education services were provided to hundreds of thousands, including Khmer, Highland Lao, Lowland Lao, and the Vietnamese boat people. IRC's commitment to the remaining refugees continues to this day as they linger in camps or return to their homeland after years in exile.

In 1988 the Burmese government violently suppressed prodemocracy demonstrations in

Throughout the 1980s IRC developed special programs for handicapped Cambodians, including classes and training for the deaf and the blind as well as for refugees with Down's syndrome.

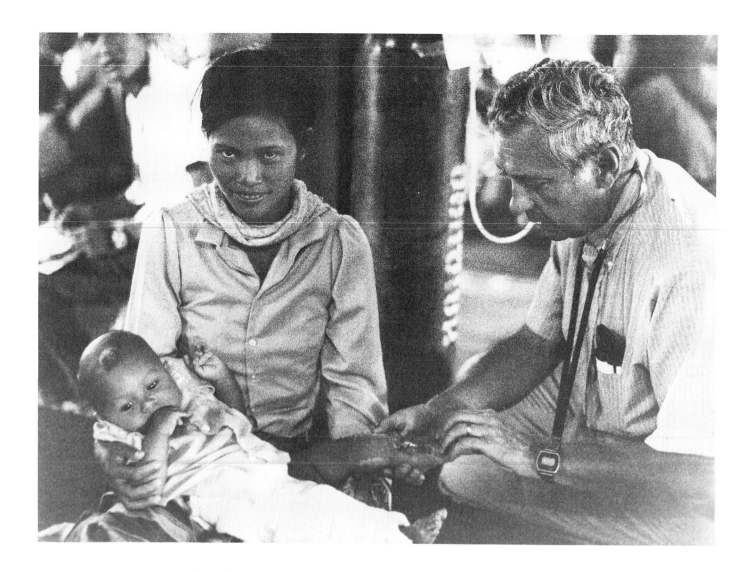

A FEW MONTHS TURN INTO A LIFETIME COMMITMENT

The opportunity for a sabbatical from his post as dean of the Dartmouth Medical School presented Dr. James C. Strickler with many possibilities. How might he spend those few months that were his to shape? The desire to help people directly, a desire that had led him to medicine as a profession, remained strong. That desire in tandem with his experience as a medical officer in southeast Asia during his tenure in the U.S. Navy prompted him to consider spending some time abroad. He began researching possibilities to spend his sabbatical working overseas.

One of the responses he received was a telephone call from Louis Wiesner at the International Rescue Committee. At the time, Dr. Strickler did not know about IRC. He was a little surprised to hear the voice at the other end of the line inquiring, "Would you like to work in a refugee camp in Thailand for a few months?" Dr. Strickler's medical expertise was certainly needed.

Soon he and his wife, Peg, were on their way to Khao-I-Dang Camp. Dr. Strickler worked as physician coordinator and in pediatric and outpatient services. Peg's skills as a teacher of English also benefited the refugees.

Dr. James C. Strickler performing one of his many daily activities in Khao-I-Dang Camp.

His experience in the camp, Strickler recalls, was not unlike working in a MASH unit. His involvement deepened as he witnessed incredible pain and loss, in this situation in which the mortality rate was a staggering 16 percent.

He returned each day to his house on stilts, exhausted but well aware that his efforts were making a difference. "I saved a life today," he would say to his wife. Again and again he thought to himself: "I am getting so much more out of this than I am giving."

Not only did the immediate scene captivate Dr. Strickler, but so too did the whole scheme of medical care for refugees. He attended monthly meetings in Bangkok organized by the United Nations and the Thai government. Complex medical issues were grappled with and solutions were sought. The professor of medicine's academic interests were stimulated and stretched.

After seven months in Khao-I-Dang, the Stricklers returned to Dartmouth College. The memories of the refugee camp remained very much alive, and soon Dr. Strickler found new ways to put his experiences to work.

IRC's country director in Thailand had been so impressed with Dr. Strickler's involvement that he recommended the doctor be made a member of the IRC board of directors. Strickler, now firmly committed to the cause of refugees, said "Count me in." Typical of the IRC board, it was not long before Strickler received another telephone call. "Can you go to Beirut?"

This was the beginning of many trips abroad. Jim Strickler has visited most every program operated by the International Rescue Committee. His involvement and commitment have continued to deepen and evolve. Today Dr. Strickler chairs the executive committee of the IRC board of directors.

The Stricklers' participation extends even further. One of their daughters, upon graduating from college, went to Thailand to volunteer some time. She is still there, working for CARE. She is married to a Thai man who works for another relief agency, Concern. Soon they will both be leaving Thailand for Cambodia, where they will assist Cambodian refugees now returning home.

▶ ▶ ▶ ▶

As refugees from Laos continued escaping to northern Thai camps, IRC expanded its work to feed the children.

and mosquito nets for Burmese refugees. Six laboratories for diagnosis and treatment, staffed by Burmese, were established. IRC also assisted with construction of housing, digging of wells, and the provision of food and basic health care. For those students who reached Bangkok, IRC helped with stipends for food, shelter, and clothing.

In April 1992 the voluntary repatriation of over three hundred thousand Khmer refugees began. By May of 1993 all but a handful of the refugees had returned to Cambodia. IRC has been a key player in the complex repatriation program for Cambodians being orchestrated by the United Nations, the largest such effort in U.N. history. IRC has established a medical, public health, and sanitation program in Kompong Chhnang and Battambang provinces inside Cambodia. Oral rehydration therapy, treatment for diarrheal diseases, and an immunization campaign are saving the lives of many children—in a country where one in five children dies of preventable disease before the age of five. The program is augmented by IRC-trained health workers who are reaching out to remote communities.

Inside Cambodia IRC is providing medicines and vaccines, medical supplies and equipment, construction materials for wells and latrines, and educational materials. At the same time that health problems are being addressed IRC is also putting into place a sustainable community health program that will continue well after the time that IRC withdraws from the region.

There is much concern about the safety and security of refugees returning home to Cambodia. The Khmer Rouge remains hostile, and the Peace Accords agreed upon in October 1991 have more than once been violated. Members of the United Nations Transitional Authority for Cambodia (UNTAC)

Rangoon, forcing more than seven thousand students to flee to remote camps along the Thailand-Burma border. Ongoing military assaults and persecution drove many more into Thailand. By the end of 1990 some twenty-seven hundred remained in malaria-infested border camps and an additional fifteen hundred lived surreptitiously in Bangkok in constant fear of arrest, detention, and deportation.

IRC initiated a malaria control program, providing medicines, equipment, blankets, have been targets of violence, and villagers have been warned against cooperating with UNTAC representatives. A senior official of the Phnom Penh government was murdered outside his home.

These events, although isolated, have cast a shadow over the success of the Khmer's return. Repatriation moves ahead, but not without apprehensions.

IRC continues to provide public health and sanitation projects in the camps along the Laos-Thailand and Burma-Thailand borders. Plans are proceeding to cut through the impasse that has long kept Lao from returning home. A strategy is being worked out that will provide either for resettlement in a third country or voluntary repatriation from Thailand to Laos.

There is much uneasiness about the prospective return of hilltribe Lao who, over the course of seventeen years, have come to depend on assistance. Basic skills have not been developed. IRC has adapted its programs to correct this disadvantage, providing intensive skills training for Lao who hope to repatriate. Agricultural training is emphasized, as is the participation of women in all projects. A drug-abuse prevention, detoxification, and rehabilitation program and a traditional medicine center are operated by Hmong who have been trained in both Western and traditional medicines. Returning

Thousands of Indochinese, including this family, were among the eleven thousand refugees resettled by IRC in the United States during 1990.

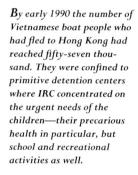

By early 1990 the number of Vietnamese boat people who had fled to Hong Kong had reached fifty-seven thousand. They were confined to primitive detention centers where IRC concentrated on the urgent needs of the children—their precarious health in particular, but school and recreational activities as well.

Lao will play a significant role in raising the living standards in Laos. IRC is committed to assisting returning refugees to develop and sustain viable communities and to eliminating any dependence on outside assistance.

More than sixty-eight thousand Burmese now live in camps along the Burma-Thailand border. Continuing violence and human-rights violations are forcing Burmese ethnic minorities and students to seek safety outside their homeland. The United Nations High Commissioner for Refugees (UNHCR) has no presence along the border because a presence, it is feared, will attract larger numbers of refugees. A small number of international agencies are allowed to provide critical assistance to the Burmese on the border.

IRC is providing emergency medical relief and food assistance to students and families living in makeshift camps. The rice and fish paste provided is supplemented by homegrown vegetables and protein from local farm animals. A public health team offers community health and sanitation services and training. A clean-water system has been developed, and shallow wells are being dug. With the help of refugee volunteers an environmental education campaign has been launched.

Among the targets of the Burmese army's terror were the Rohingyas, a Muslim ethnic minority considered unwanted. In 1992 thousands of Rohingya Muslims fled into Bangladesh. Nearly three hundred thousand are now there. The Bangladeshis have

As the flow of Cambodian refugees returning to their homeland increased during 1992, IRC went inside Cambodia with them. The installation of shallow wells to provide clean water was one of the projects carried out by IRC specialists.

been as generous as their extremely limited resources allow; it is already one of the world's poorest countries. But much assistance has been needed for these displaced people. IRC dispatched a team of sanitarians to the area where the Rohingya refugees gathered. Latrine systems have been erected in the camps, helping to prevent epidemics.

Over the past two decades some two million people have fled from Vietnam, Cambodia, and Laos. By the end of 1991 more than one million had been admitted to the United States. IRC's resettlement work, carried out in sixteen domestic offices, has led to the effective absorption of over 120,000 Indochinese refugees into the nation's social, economic, and cultural life.

The International Rescue Committee remains committed to assisting refugees and the displaced in southeast Asia as well as to helping assimilate newly arriving refugees into life in the United States.

Thousands Flee Castro's Cuba

▶ ▶ ▶ ▶ ▶ ▶ ▶ ▶ ▶ ▶

Thousands fled Cuba following Castro's takeover in 1959. Most headed for the United States. During the first three years of the dictatorship, some 225,000 refugees fled. All but 35,000 received asylum in the United States.

Within a month of Castro's seizing power, two representatives of the International Rescue Committee were on the scene: chairman Leo Cherne and H. William Fitelson, a lifelong student of revolutionary movements and an IRC board member since 1946. Fitelson met with several of Castro's "lieutenants" who were making a break from the totalitarian movement. Although fearful of imprisonment or execution, they spoke bluntly about the new regime that they had looked to with hope as Batista was overthrown.

It was immediately clear to both Fitelson and Cherne that a major refugee flow was imminent. In the fall of 1959 IRC's board of directors pledged assistance to Cuban refugees, and in 1960 IRC's Caribbean Refugee Program was established.

This program served not only Cuban refugees but also people escaping the oppressive Trujillo regime in the Dominican Republic and Papa Doc's Haiti. The International Rescue Committee provided relief services, family reunion assistance, and legal aid to dissident Haitian exiles escaping the Duvalier dictatorship and was a founding member of the National Emergency Coalition for Haitian Refugees. As Cuban jails filled up with democratic-minded dissidents, IRC intensified its human rights advocacy efforts.

On May 1, 1961, Castro announced that Cuba was a "socialist country." There was, he declared, no need for elections. By December he was proclaiming, "I absolutely believe in Marxism."

America began experiencing something entirely new. Never before had the United States been the place of first asylum for so many political refugees. The chairman of IRC's Caribbean Refugee Program, Nicholas Duke Biddle, commented:

> We are dealing with people who have lost a great deal more than their material possessions. They can be our allies and advocates at a time when we need maximum support in the Western Hemisphere. This can be so only if their exile does not become an experience to be recalled in the future with bitterness and with memories of indifference and lack of understanding on our part.

Among those helped by IRC was the Cuban pilot who stowed away on a commercial airplane. Like thousands of others, he arrived in Florida, the logical port of first call for the vast

Soon after Fidel Castro assumed power in Cuba in 1959, he established a dictatorship based on large-scale imprisonment and execution of democratic-minded citizens.

As Castro's repression intensified, thousands of Cubans escaped to Florida by boats, rafts, and anything that might float.

majority of Cuban, Haitian, and Dominican refugees. IRC assisted him with clothes, housing, and employment. He worked and saved until he was able to buy plane tickets for his family, who soon joined him.

A worker who refused to serve in Castro's Revolutionary Militia teamed up with seven other men and two women and headed for Florida in a small outboard-motor boat. A few miles from their destination they were caught in a gale and blown back out to sea. They lost sight of land and ran out of food and water. They had all but abandoned hope after three days of being tossed at sea when the crew of a merchant ship spotted them. The Coast Guard was radioed and the refugees were soon brought to safety.

In 1965 Castro surprised the world by announcing that Cubans who desired to leave were free to do so. President Johnson accepted the challenge by opening wide the doors to the United States. In December of that year the Cuban airlift began. For the next five years Cubans arrived at a rate of forty thousand each month. Flight from Veradero Beach to Miami continued until Castro

reversed his earlier decision, no longer permitting the exodus. IRC was actively involved in helping to resettle the thousands of refugees building new lives in America.

IRC's resettlement program focused on bringing together families that had been separated during flight. IRC vice president Betsy Landreth went to Florida and volunteered countless days as a one-woman missing persons bureau. Contacts made through police departments around the country became her primary resource. "Cops are the best," she reported. "They know where to look. I know them all by now." Her ingenuity and the cooperative spirit she engendered led to the happy reunion of hundreds of refugee families.

The Cuban-American community, nearly all refugees themselves, did much to assist newly arriving fellow citizens. A one-night telethon raised $2 million in aid that was distributed by IRC. IRC board members Nena Goodman, Sophie Gimbel, Betsy Landreth, and Dolores Smithies were leaders in the Cuban refugee cause.

In Miami, Freedom House was the way station where IRC and other agencies registered Cuban refugees prior to resettlement in their new communities throughout the United States.

FREEDOM HOUSE

Two other destinations for Cuban refugees were Spain and Mexico, the only countries maintaining air service with Havana. Spain was liberal in granting visas to Cuban nationals and, despite its own despotic government, became a way station on the road to freedom.

In 1969 IRC president William J. vanden Heuvel recounted "one man's compulsive hunger for freedom." He wrote:

Two young Cubans hid in a wheel compart-ment of a jet airliner going from Havana to Spain. The temperature during the nine-hour flight was 40 degrees below zero, and oxygen was almost nonexistent in the tiny, unpressur-ized and unheated wheel pod. Doctors say that ordinarily a man can retain consciousness for about three minutes under such conditions, and live for only a short while thereafter.

Reuniting family members who had been separated in flight from Cuba was central to IRC's resettlement work.

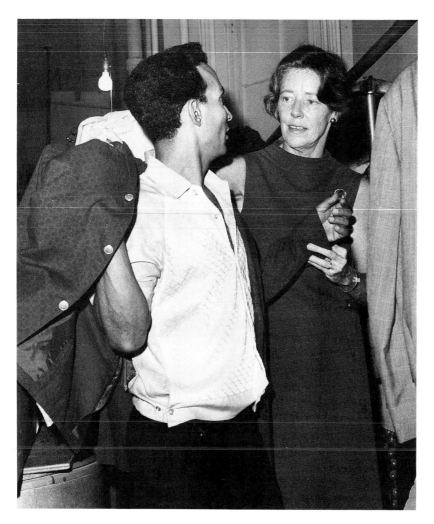

When the plane approached Madrid, one of the Cuban youths fell into the sea and vanished. The other one dropped from the wheel casing when the plane landed—unconscious but alive. In a few hours he regained consciousness and eventually recovered from his ordeal—a case which doctors termed "an unparalleled and unexplainable miracle." When asked why he had taken such an incredible risk, the new refugee replied, "I was looking for a better world and a new future." He asked repeatedly and tearfully whether he would be sent back to Cuba.

Soon this seventeen-year-old refugee was in the United States, sponsored by the International Rescue Committee.

Who were these thousands of Cuban refugees? A random sampling of 750 IRC cases showed that 15 percent were professionals and 12 percent were business people; 27 percent were white-collar workers and more than 35 percent were skilled and unskilled workers; 7 percent were small shop owners, 2 percent were farmers, and the remaining 2 percent were "other." Clearly, the refugees represented all of Cuba.

ABOVE:

The Cuban clothing center in New York was organized and staffed by volunteers, including Betsy Landreth, an IRC board member. The center provided clothing for newly arrived refugees.

RIGHT:

IRC resettlement caseworkers in New York made it possible for thousands of Cubans to start new lives in freedom.

Like all refugees, the Cubans hoped their exile would be brief. But unfolding events at home tempered their dreams. By 1962 it was no surprise to learn that Soviet troops were digging in and missile launchers were being built.

An unexpected outcome of the Cuban refugee exodus was the attention it brought to Haitian refugees, victims of savage persecutions by the Duvaliers, both father and son. Haitians were dismissed as "economic migrants" rather than legitimate refugees fleeing oppression and government brutality.

Since the early 1960s the International Rescue Committee had been expressing its concern about Haitian refugees and helping many of them to resettle. Legal, material, and family reunion services were provided. A group of Haitians who had escaped to the Bahamas were granted asylum in the United

François "Papa Doc" Duvalier's reign of terror in Haiti, which created a constant flight of refugees, was perpetuated by his son, "Baby Doc," who inherited his father's title, President-for-Life.

States through efforts of IRC. IRC also conducted a ten-day legal fight to block the extradition of 116 Haitian sailors who had revolted against the Duvalier regime and made their way to Miami.

Haitians who had escaped to the Dominican Republic and other nearby islands were provided basic services as well as guidance about immigration law. IRC was the principal agency receiving Haitians who made their escape to the United States. Their numbers were small in comparison to the thousands fleeing Cuba. But the Haitians were the "poorest of the poor," as IRC described them, with the fewest friends. IRC's vigilance kept them alive and in the

During the early 1960s many Haitian refugees fled to the Dominican Republic, where IRC helped them survive.

At Kennedy Airport, IRC executive director Carel Sternberg welcomes a group of Haitian sailors who defected to the United States.

public eye while battles over deportation and adjustment of status were being waged.

Horrible episodes occurred while policy was being debated and hairs were being split over the distinction between a refugee and an "economic migrant." Particularly appalling was an event involving one small band of the many mercenary smugglers who demanded as much as $500 per head to bring desperate refugees to safety. These smugglers did not, however, always deliver on their promises. Florida police watched from the shore as passengers within sight of freedom were tossed into the sea. Ten people were rescued, but five children and a pregnant mother drowned.

In 1970 a group of Haitian sailors who had attempted to overthrow Duvalier escaped to the U.S. Naval Base at Guantanamo. Eventually they arrived in Miami, where they were granted asylum. IRC assumed responsibility for them, arranging for housing and other essential needs. Most of the sailors were resettled in New York, where intensive efforts resulted in gainful employment for the refugees.

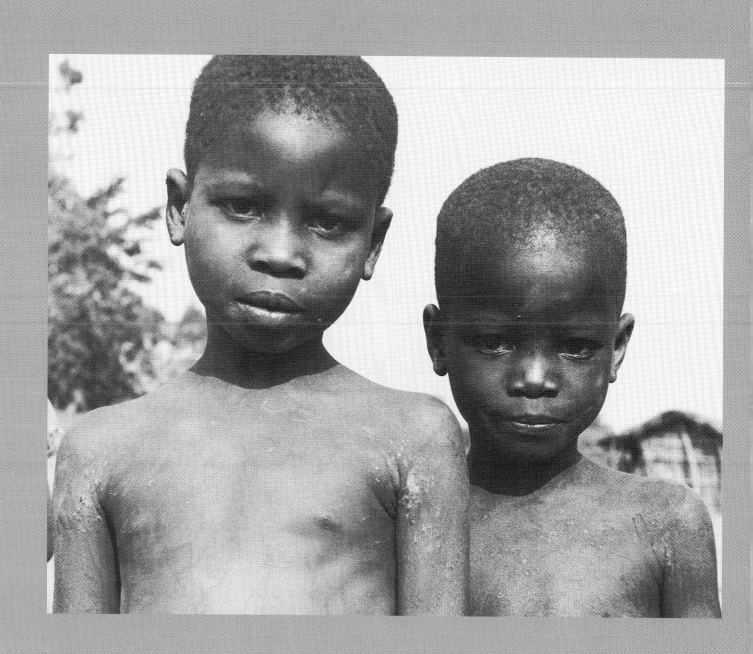

African Nations Struggle for Independence

▶ ▶ ▶ ▶ ▶ ▶ ▶ ▶ ▶ ▶

The International Rescue Committee witnessed many crises on the African continent during the decade of the 1960s. Transitions from colonial governments did not always lead to peace. Internal conflicts often forced large numbers of innocent people to flee civil strife and new oppressive regimes.

When over two hundred thousand Angolans escaped the Portuguese colonial government and fled to nearby Zaire in 1962, IRC was there. This was IRC's first initiative on the African continent. IRC supplied medicines and enlisted refugee doctors for a medical assistance program. Dr. Marcus Wooley, a French-speaking surgeon who had himself once been a refugee from Haiti, was recruited for service in Zaire. He administered the distribution of medical supplies donated by the American pharmaceutical industry. He also performed surgery at the Service d'Assistance aux Refugies Angolais clinic and the many border camps he visited. He devoted much of his time to teaching first aid and preventive care to the refugees and to improving the knowledge and skills of Angolan nurses and medical technicians.

Mounting tensions in Zaire made the work of IRC staff extremely perilous. The threat of troops, both government and insurgent, intensified. America's concern and compassion for Africa also increased. Together with Catholic Relief Services and Church World Service, IRC was able to send $179,000 worth of drugs and medicines, beds and medical equipment, and high-protein food to aid the Angolan refugees. After eighteen months Dr. Wooley returned to the United States. His replacement, also a Haitian refugee physician, was unable to remain in Zaire very long. Deteriorating security and the withdrawal of U.N. troops forced the doctor to depart. Fortunately, local personnel had by that time been well trained to manage the programs initiated by IRC.

In 1964 IRC also moved into Botswana, a country where a large number of refugees from South Africa had congregated. An important part of the program was preparing young people to enter schools in Tanzania and Zambia. Many South Africans and refugees from what was then Rhodesia had fled to Zambia and Kenya, where IRC initiated programs.

In Nigeria the Ibos had become a very successful group of business people. Suddenly they found themselves threatened by a more numerous and resentful tribe. As dangers escalated, the Ibos retreated to their tribal lands, proclaiming in 1967 the independent nation of Biafra. Civil war and massacres followed.

IRC joined with other organizations in launching the Biafra Christmas Ship that provided three thousand tons of food, drugs, and other life-saving supplies to the Ibos. IRC also recruited

IRC's first involvement in Africa was in 1962, when two hundred thousand refugees fled to Zaire from the repressive Portuguese colonial government of Angola. As in all major refugee flows, the children especially needed IRC's care.

RIGHT:

Angolan women were in desperate need of relief and medical services in Zaire.

BELOW:

Dr. Marc Wooley, a Haitian who himself had been resettled by IRC, headed the IRC medical program in Zaire ministering to the two hundred thousand Angolan refugees.

Nigerian doctors in the United States for volunteer missions to Biafra. At first it seemed that Biafra might survive. But famine and the superior army of Nigeria's central government overcame the struggle for independence. The Ibos surrendered in 1970, but not before an estimated one million people had died.

The magnitude of the crisis in Biafra captured the world's attention. Several other conflicts on the African continent were hardly noticed by the general public, but IRC was working in many regions, assisting refugees from Angola, Sudan, Guinea, and Mozambique. Ever-growing numbers and needs led IRC to realize that it would soon be facing

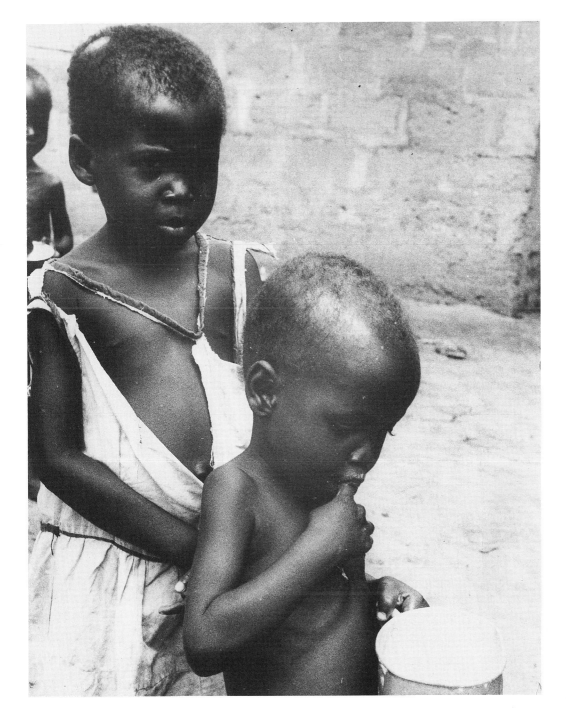

The bloody 1968 civil war in Nigeria resulted in massive numbers of sick and hungry Biafrans, most of them children. IRC participated in the relief effort and sent a team of physicians to combat disease and starvation.

increasing responsibilities in Africa. An IRC report stated:

> Refugee problems in Africa will undoubtedly multiply and intensify as the result of complex tribal, religious, racial, national, and political conflicts. Biafra is an extreme example, but it would be unrealistic not to expect more crises in this developing continent where so many new nations are groping for identity and survival. IRC's commitment to the refugee cause will require a deepening of its involvement in Africa.

Escape from China

▶ ▶ ▶ ▶ ▶ ▶ ▶ ▶ ▶ ▶

The International Rescue Committee was needed in another part of the world as the stream of refugees leaving mainland China for Hong Kong became a flood. The exodus had begun in 1949 when Mao Tse-tung seized power. By 1961 Hong Kong's population had reached 3,300,000; in 1946 it had been six hundred thousand.

It was in May 1962 that a photographer in Hong Kong turned his lens on Li Ying, dejected and weeping, as she was pushed back toward Red China. She was forced to give up the freedom she thought she had finally reached. Li Ying was one of at least sixty thousand others caught in the same plight.

IRC president William J. vanden Heuvel went to Hong Kong that same May. Those who had escaped and avoided deportation were in immediate need of basic care and sustenance. IRC arranged to distribute food and clothing, and hostels were set up as temporary shelter for those with no family or friends to turn to.

Whatever skills or training the refugees had was put to use in Hong Kong, and many were given vocational training. The boom in tourism in Hong Kong led IRC to open a hotel training school. The Hong Kong Hotel Association cooperated in administering the school and in placing graduates. The China Refugee Development Organization, a self-help project, kept thousands of refugee artists and craftspeople employed.

IRC also helped professionals maintain accreditation in their fields. Many refugee doctors were sent to England for postgraduate study. The majority of these doctors returned to Hong Kong to work in clinics under the aegis of the Medical and Health Department of the Crown Colony.

There was a pressing need for day care, to enable both parents or single parents to work. In cooperation with Hong Kong's social welfare department, IRC opened its first day nursery in 1963. The success of the center led to the opening of several additional day nurseries, enabling refugee mothers to work. Children at the centers were immunized and given nutritional supplements. The girls and boys, ranging in ages from two to seven, were regularly examined by refugee physicians and given appropriate medical care.

IRC's international appeal for individuals and families to sponsor children brought a generous response from Belgium, the United Kingdom, and the United States. Contributions covered the costs of each child in the nurseries and made possible the opening of additional day care centers.

The exodus of refugees from mainland China to Hong Kong started in 1949 when Mao Tse-tung seized power. By 1961 the refugee population had reached 3,300,000. The following year IRC started its work in Hong Kong.

Chinese refugees fled by boat (above) and thousands more swam to Hong Kong through the treacherous waters separating mainland China and Hong Kong (right). Countless freedom swimmers drowned in their effort to escape and others were killed by sharks. Many of the teenage survivors were sheltered in an IRC hostel.

In the photograph, a sign reads: INTERNATIONAL RESCUE COMMITTEE IG-METALL DAY NURSE[RY] 國際救援會西德五金公會托兒所

IRC established nurseries and day care centers for the children of Chinese refugees who had escaped to Hong Kong, enabling parents to work and become self-supporting.

IRC provided balanced meals as well as schooling, recreation, and training in basic hygiene for Chinese refugee children.

Another area of activity for IRC in Hong Kong was overseas resettlement. IRC strongly advocated a change in America's Chinese exclusion policy, and President Kennedy did raise the quota from a token 105 to 10,000 over a two-year period. IRC also worked to resettle Chinese refugees in other parts of the free world, including Taiwan, Canada, Brazil, and other Latin American countries.

The Cultural Revolution led by Mao Tse-tung accelerated in the late 1960s. Each persecutory convulsion forced out another wave of refugees. The easiest way to escape was on fishing boats. Scenes of desperate refugees adrift on rafts and in small boats were relayed around the world—scenes that would be repeated a decade later along the coast of Vietnam. Despite stepped-up patrols, at least seventeen thousand Chinese escaped in 1968 alone.

The IRC office in Hong Kong enabled qualified Chinese refugees to resettle in the United States, Canada, and other free countries. Deanna Chu (right) was greeted by her sister, Barbara, on her arrival in San Francisco.

Back to China. In 1980 the Crown Colony of Hong Kong initiated a tough deportation policy, imprisoning all refugees who were apprehended and then returning them against their will to China. Even children reaching Hong Kong to join their parents were forcibly deported.

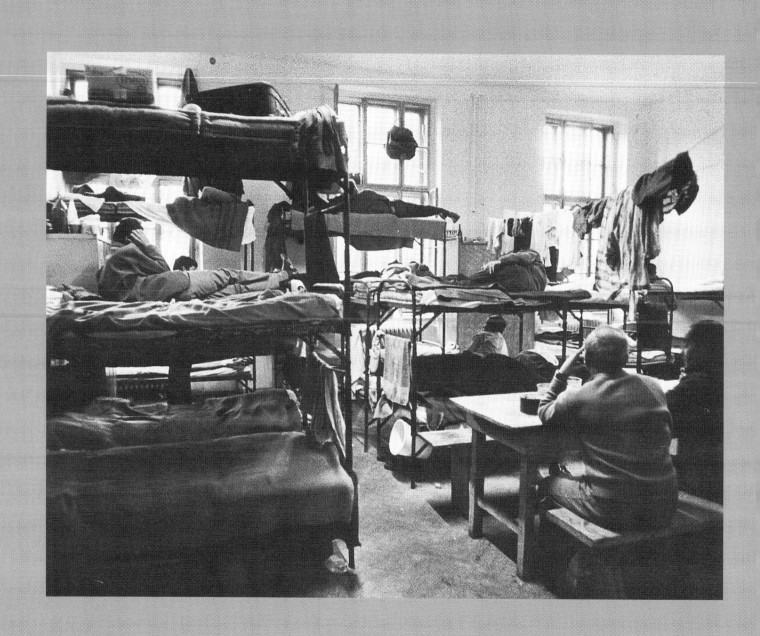

Behind the Iron Curtain
the Fight for Freedom Continues

▶ ▶ ▶ ▶ ▶ ▶ ▶ ▶ ▶ ▶

Oppression in central and Eastern Europe continued to force freedom seekers isolated by the Iron Curtain to pull up roots and move on. Waves of refugees made their way to IRC offices in Vienna or Paris, Munich or Geneva, Madrid or Rome. In 1964 alone at least forty thousand refugees passed through Western Europe on their way to a place of first asylum. An increasing number expressed interest in staying in Europe rather than resettling in the United States or Canada or Australia.

World War II had ended twenty years earlier, but even as the last vestiges of the war were being swept away, new crises erupted to disturb the quiet. In 1968 the crisis occurred in Czechoslovakia. On August 21 the Soviets stormed Czechoslovakia to put an end to the Prague Spring, which was unleashing an exuberant spirit of freedom. By the time Alexander Dubček became president in January 1968, a heady breeze was blowing throughout Czechoslovakia. But Soviet tanks moved in to crush the peaceful revolution, and the Kremlin issued its Brezhnev Doctrine, which in effect stated, "Once a Communist country, always a Communist country." Dubček and his comrades were forcibly taken to Moscow, mass arrests began, and thousands began voting with their feet. Fifty thousand Czechs and Slovaks fled to Austria, France, Belgium, Italy, the Netherlands, Scandinavia, and the United States.

Soon IRC found itself responsible for more than fourteen thousand refugees, including many students and intellectuals, who were particular targets of the Soviet regime. What had been learned during the Hungarian crisis of 1956 was put to use as assistance programs for the Czech and Slovak refugees were established.

Once again refugee settlements cropped up all over Europe. The year 1968 had already seen large numbers of Romanians, Hungarians, and Poles streaming out of their homelands. Restless Polish students, inspired by student activism in America, declared their discontent. The Polish press and media responded with an anti-Zionist campaign, forcing most of the Polish Jews who had survived Hitler's extermination crusade to flee.

In 1967, while events in central and Eastern Europe dominated the headlines, a military junta in Greece established a dictatorship. The civilian government was overthrown, democratic

Crowded, barrack-like rooms in refugee camps accommodated new waves of people escaping from Eastern Europe during the 1960s. IRC offices in Austria, France, Germany, Italy, Sweden, and Switzerland provided relief and resettlement services for the refugees seeking to rebuild their lives.

A rising tide of asylum
seekers fled from Czecho-
slovakia in 1968 when Soviet
forces extinguished the
people's bid for more
freedom. IRC established
language-training classes
for many of the young
refugees to prepare them
for resettlement.

leaders were imprisoned, and citizens fled. Over a period of seven years hundreds of Greek refugees were helped by IRC, primarily in France but also in Austria and Germany. In 1974 the dictatorship in Greece collapsed and the refugees were able to return home. The General Assembly of the Franc-Hellenci movement in Paris announced:

Our members would like to express their gratitude and convey their warmest thanks to IRC for the assistance which your organization has extended to Greek democratic victims of the military dictatorship. You have met and helped a number of Greek democrats, and there have been some desperate cases who were saved only thanks to your assistance. We are most grateful and deeply moved by the interest and understanding that you have shown.

The New Nation of Bangladesh Emerges

▷ ▷ ▷ ▷ ▷ ▷ ▷ ▷ ▷ ▷

The world witnessed a refugee flight of unprecedented numbers in 1971, when the Bengali people of East Pakistan sought independence from an oppressive government two thousand miles to the west. With terrifying thoroughness the Pakistani army swept through the country to crush the democratic hopes of the people. Two hundred thousand were massacred in the first assaults alone.

The world watched as ten million refugees began their flight to freedom—the largest mass migration in human history. Mostly Hindus in a Muslim-dominated society, they fled to India, a country already plagued with incredible poverty.

Word received at IRC headquarters made it clear that the first targets of this terror were intellectuals and professional people. Bloody details began to emerge: on a single day in March, everyone on the campus of the University of Dacca had been executed.

IRC dispatched a fact-finding mission headed by Angier Duke to camps growing up near Calcutta. Board members Lee Thaw and Morton Hamburg were part of this mission, as was Dr. Daniel Wiener, who later became chairman of IRC's medical committee. Plans were made to begin an emergency relief program as quickly as possible. The team learned that the refugees had already set up a skeletal government-in-exile whose first priority was to register all medical personnel who had made their way safely to India.

Exiled physicians, nurses, teachers, and other professionals were recruited by IRC for a large-scale survival program. As is so often the case, the vast majority of refugees were women and children.

IRC's immediate action let loose a wave of generosity in the United States. IRC board member Mary Pillsbury Lord, who later served as president, soon left for India. She and her husband, Oswald, had visited virtually every refugee population that had emerged since World War II. She was described by IRC colleagues in India as an indefatigable source of hope and cheer for the refugees and volunteers. Mrs. Lord had a special talent for communicating with the refugee children across language barriers. Three Yale graduates who were serving as IRC volunteers have told how they were startled one day to hear shouts of "boola boola" in a remote corner of the globe: as they rounded a corner, they discovered Mary Lord leading a parade of refugee children chanting the Yale fight song. In Bangladesh today there are undoubtedly a few people who can recall playing soccer and singing the Yale song with an American lady named Mrs. Lord.

The ten million East Pakistani refugees who fled to India in 1971 sought shelter wherever they could, including in these drainage pipes near Calcutta.

*O*utside Calcutta, tent cities
proliferated, providing
shelter for the uprooted
people from East Pakistan.

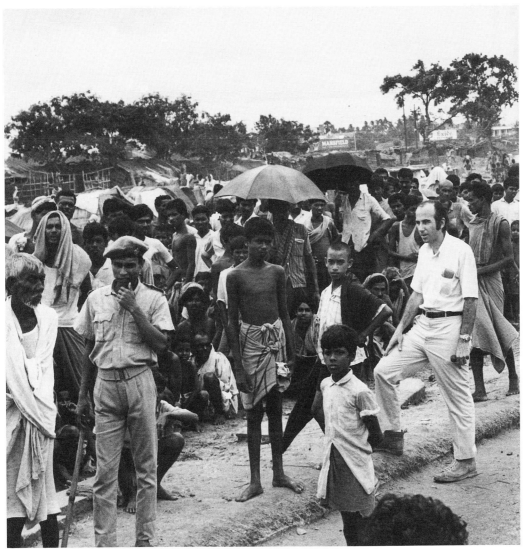

TOP, LEFT:

An emergency mission of IRC board members, headed by Angier Duke, rushed to India to investigate the most urgent needs of the refugees and to initiate relief programs.

TOP, RIGHT:

Board member Lee Thaw, seen here with Mother Theresa, had a major role in the development of IRC's medical and educational work for the refugees.

LEFT:

Dr. Daniel Wiener served as medical advisor for the IRC mission to India.

Mary Lord's longstanding commitment to the International Rescue Committee lives on in many ways, most importantly through the work of her son, Winston, who is vice chairman of the IRC board of directors. Winston Lord, a former U.S. ambassador to the People's Republic of China, is on temporary leave from board service, having been called to Washington by President Clinton to serve as assistant secretary of state for East Asia and the Pacific.

Board member Lee Thaw provided expert supervision of IRC's work in India for the months ahead. With remarkable energy and an exceptional ability to motivate people, she recruited the necessary personnel, visited camps, established contact with government officials, and persuaded camp commandants to allocate space for IRC facilities.

Thaw's reports to IRC headquarters described what seemed to be insurmountable hurdles: emergency shelter was in short supply; India had been depleted of tents and

Hundreds of makeshift clinics and dispensaries were put up by IRC. Doctors, nurses, and paramedics among the refugees themselves were recruited by IRC to staff the facilities.

tarpaulin; sanitary conditions were nonexistent in many areas where masses of refugees had congregated; fuel for cooking rice, the basis of the refugees' diet, became a problem as the landscape was stripped of trees. Unhealthy, hollow-cheeked refugees were recognizable even amidst the severe poverty of India. Despite incredible odds, IRC staff and volunteers established a successful relief program.

Board members Margery and Aaron Levenstein joined Lee Thaw in India and continued the work she had begun. Aaron pioneered a program in which former government officials of East Pakistan, now idle while in exile, were employed. Plans were laid for what would become the new nation of Bangladesh. When Bangladesh became a reality, it was no surprise that virtually every member of the new national government was a graduate of the IRC training program.

In a clinic at Barasat forty-seven medics working around the clock were treating five

hundred sick, wounded, and malnourished patients each day by the summer of 1971. An outpatient dispensary established there became a model for others that soon sprang up in several refugee camps. IRC placed 218 medical personnel in twenty-eight locations and treated over 250,000 patients each month.

A maternity center and a hospital for children were also set up at Barasat. For the children's hospital a cow shed with room for a hundred patients was made available. Its tin roof and concrete floor were considered luxurious by the many doctors working elsewhere in ankle-deep mud. A trough once used by cattle now held mothers cradling their children.

IRC collaborated with the All-India Institute of Medical Science in a research and treatment program at several nutrition therapy centers. IRC also worked closely with other relief agencies, such as Catholic Relief Services, the International Red Cross, Lutheran World Relief, and British-based Oxfam on many projects.

IRC's top priority was its medical program, but the intellectual base of what was once East Pakistan also had to be preserved. Ten thousand teachers—those who had survived attempts to eradicate the education system of East Pakistan—were recruited by IRC. A research faculty-in-exile was organized with a nucleus of 150 college instructors. Like the medical staff, the teachers were preparing for the time when their new nation would need their services as well as the talents of those they were teaching.

LEFT:

Special medical centers for the refugee children were built by IRC, among them this clinic converted from a cow shed. IRC also established hundreds of schools for the children in the crowded camps.

BOTTOM, LEFT:

Professor Aaron Levenstein lectured frequently to academicians among the refugees.

BOTTOM, RIGHT:

In the summer of 1971 IRC board member Margery Levenstein (left) and president Mary P. Lord went to the refugee camps in India. Their reports led to a further expansion of IRC's work for the East Pakistanis.

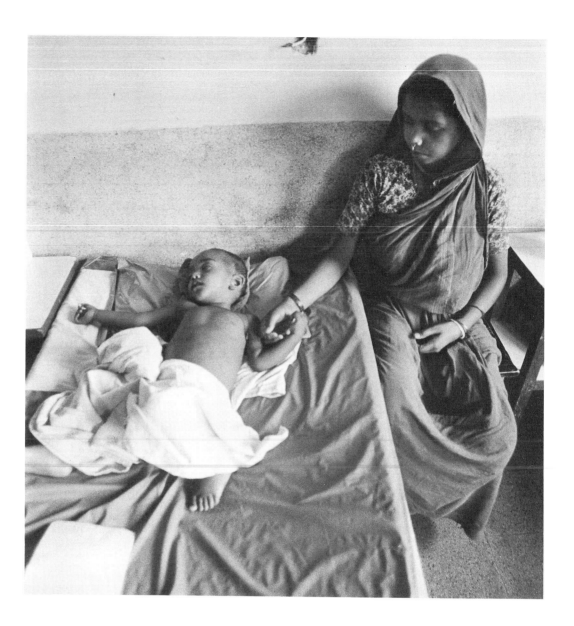

Makeshift classrooms were set up for refugee children. The schools became signs of hope for the future.

While programs moved ahead in India, IRC endeavored to alert the American public to the enormity of the crisis taking place, preparing the world for the day when the refugees would begin building a free and independent new nation. That day was not far off. By December 1971 the independent nation of Bangladesh had replaced East Pakistan. Now free but devastated and impoverished, Bangladesh needed IRC's help.

The health care network set up in the refugee camps was transferred to Bangladesh. More than seventy medical clinics were established around the country, staffed by some 250 doctors, nurses, pharmacists, and paramedics. In Dacca, the new capital of Bangladesh, IRC established a manufacturing facility that provided the intravenous fluid needed to combat cholera. A letter from the director of the Bangladesh Health Services stated:

> The installation of the i.v. fluid plant at the Institute of Public Health is a milestone in the history of production of life-saving medicines.

In early 1972 the ten million refugees in India began returning to their newly liberated nation, Bangladesh. IRC initiated extensive rehabilitation programs for them, setting up clinics and a center to combat the ravages of cholera.

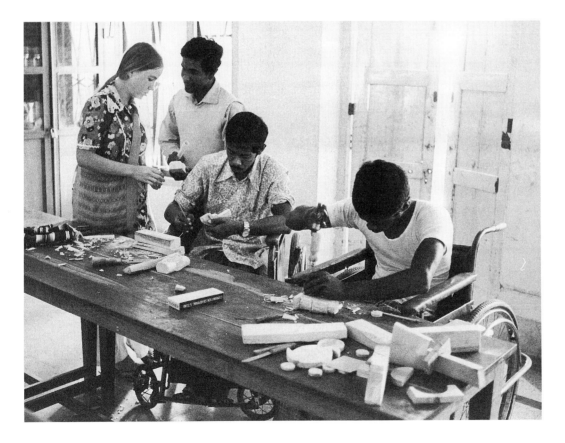

Vocational training and special projects for war-wounded people were among the rehabilitation efforts conducted by IRC in Bangladesh.

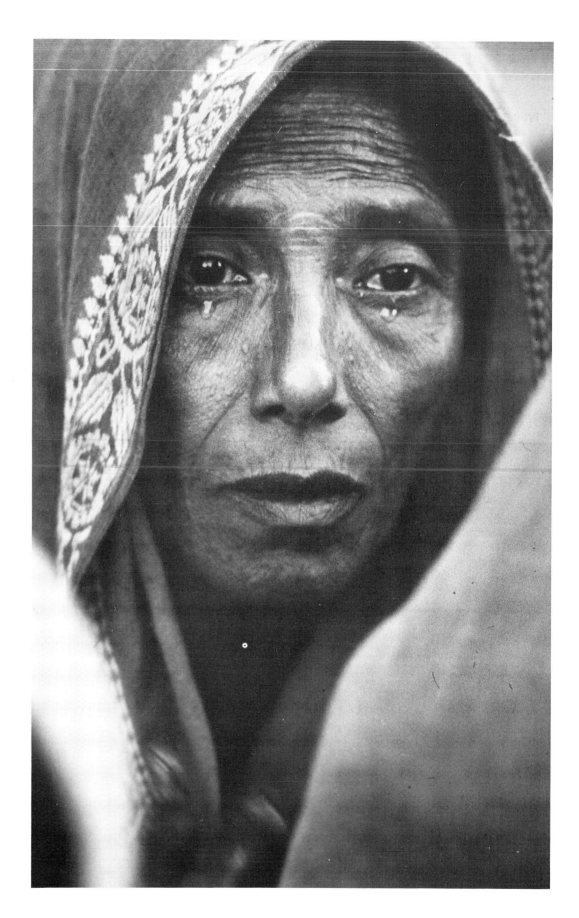

For war-widowed women of Bangladesh IRC established special centers where self-sufficiency skills were taught, giving them a measure of financial independence.

Without the active support and assistance from the International Rescue Committee, it would not have been possible to install this plant. This humanitarian service is a shining example from which millions of people in Bangladesh will derive benefit.

IRC programs were carried out in close cooperation with Bangladesh organizations, including the renowned Cholera Research Laboratory, where IRC supported and trained medical professionals. Vocational rehabilitation programs were designed for those disabled during the war, and an education program for young people provided scholarships for more than seventeen thousand students eager to continue their studies. Other ventures included a fishermen's co-operative that helped reestablish fishing as an important industry for the country.

One of the greatest tragedies of the fight for independence was the rape by soldiers of thousands of women. Considered forever dishonored, the women were no longer accepted by their families. Also in need of help were widows with no families. Centers were established where self-sufficiency skills were taught, according the women some independence.

By 1975 all IRC programs in Bangladesh had been successfully transferred to local groups. The work initiated by IRC was carried on by the people of the new nation of Bangladesh.

Turmoil in Chile Forces Out Thousands

▶ ▶ ▶ ▶ ▶ ▶ ▶ ▶ ▶ ▶

In 1973, after enjoying forty years of democracy, Chile suddenly suffered political upheaval. Augusto Pinochet Ugarte began systematically crushing all expressions of political freedom. The press was censored, the right of assembly was denied, labor unions were disbanded, countless individuals were jailed and tortured, and many more "disappeared." Dissension in any form was not tolerated.

Early in 1974 IRC sent one of its most experienced volunteer leaders to Chile. Cecil Lyon had had a long and distinguished career in the foreign service, including serving as U.S. ambassador to Chile. Now, as an IRC board member, he was returning to Chile to investigate the possibility of helping victims of the oppressive Pinochet regime.

Lyon quickly learned that the last few years in Chile had been chaotic. President Salvador Allende, whom Pinochet had overthrown, had exercised extensive controls, and many were happy to see him go. But already people seemed aware of impending oppression under Pinochet.

Although Chile was a predominantly middle-class country, the new regime was aligning itself only with the upper class. Thousands were dismissed from their jobs. Thousands more were imprisoned. Hundreds of Communists, as well as social democrats and other liberals, had already made their way out, first to Argentina, then on to Sweden and France, Switzerland and Austria, Belgium and the Netherlands.

While pressing for the admission of Chileans into the United States, IRC began assisting those who had reached places of asylum. Health and nutrition programs were begun in regions of Argentina and Peru, where refugees were gathering in large numbers.

It was not until December 1975, more than two years after Pinochet took control, that the first Chilean refugees began arriving in the United States.

Resettlement was difficult. For the Chileans there was no community of fellow nationals already in the United States. Barriers of language and culture were hard to overcome. The American economy was weak. Jobs were not plentiful. Many Chileans had suffered extreme physical and psychological torture, and there were wounds to heal. With the assistance of IRC and the generosity of the American people, many Chileans were able to begin new lives. Throughout the 1970s refugees from other oppressive Latin American countries, including Uruguay, Paraguay, and Guatemala, sought asylum and were assisted by IRC. Volunteer doctors, nurses, teachers, and social workers provided critical support for IRC programs.

General Augusto Pinochet's military dictatorship of Chile in 1973 stamped out all semblance of democratic thought, in spite of a protest by the Catholic Bishops of Chile that "no man or woman can be subject to physical torture, humiliation, or terror." IRC sponsored the resettlement of hundreds of the refugees granted asylum, in concert with Amnesty International, Christian and Jewish congregations, and other human rights groups.

Masses on the Move in Africa

▶ ▶ ▶ ▶ ▶ ▶ ▶ ▶ ▶ ▶

The world witnessed unimaginable cruelty in Uganda in 1971 as Idi Amin's troops carried out his brutal genocidal directives. Among those who suffered the most were Asian nationals, especially Indians, descendants of those brought by the British at the turn of the century to build the Kenya-Uganda Railway.

Amin's reckless looting of Uganda had thrown the economy into chaos. He needed a scapegoat, and he chose the Asian minority, who had become productive members of the middle class. They had important roles in Uganda's trade, factories, plantations, and industry. They were accountants and managers, doctors and lawyers, teachers and engineers. In August 1972 Amin began forcing them to flee, announcing that God had instructed him to do so. Once they were out, Amin seized their property and goods.

A hurriedly organized airlift transported several thousand Ugandan refugees to Austria, Belgium, England, Italy, Malta, and Spain. Two thousand were allowed to enter the United States. IRC helped many of them resettle. With the help of Asian communities and student groups, homes were found for the refugees in several cities around the country. In 1974 additional Ugandan refugees were allowed entry into the United States, and IRC helped reunite many family members who had been separated by Amin's savagery.

In 1977 persecuted Ugandans started pouring into Kenya. Those forced out this time were indigenous and professional people, especially teachers, physicians, and nurses. The United Nations reported: "By the scale and capriciousness of its official murder, Uganda is in a class by itself." IRC opened a clinic in Nairobi, staffed by refugees. Soon the clinic was treating more than sixty people each day, at least half of them children. IRC recruited medical personnel for hospitals outside Nairobi, in locales where refugees were gathering. In addition IRC helped many Ugandans to continue their education even while living in exile. Schools were opened, staffed, and supplied, and fellowships were established at several universities in Africa.

Kenya's refugee population exploded as thousands streamed in from South Africa, Namibia, what was then Rhodesia, Mozambique, Rwanda, Sudan, Ethiopia, and Somalia.

Leo Cherne hurried to Nairobi, where he met with Kinga Wamwendia, the head of the Joint Refugee Services of Kenya (JRSK). Political upheaval and racial persecution in many regions of Africa were forcing huge numbers of people to use the only weapon they had: flight.

At Kennedy Airport IRC greeted the first group of Ugandan refugees admitted to the United States. The year before, in 1972, Idi Amin had announced his intention to expel all Asian nationals from Uganda.

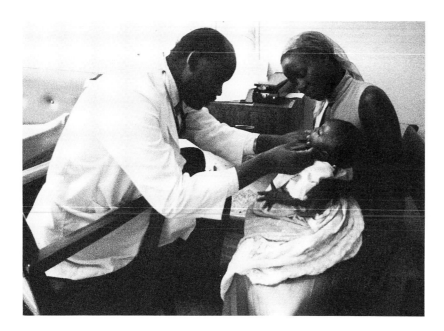

As Idi Amin's bloody oppression intensified, an increasing number of Ugandans sought asylum in Kenya, where IRC provided medical care, education, vocational training, and child care programs for the refugees.

At Cherne's recommendation, the IRC board of directors authorized the establishment of a major clinic with a full-time professional staff. The clinic, operated in cooperation with the JRSK, was a sign of hope amidst incredible pain and loss—for the woman in labor, the young widow in her eighth month of pregnancy, the mother and child who had not slept in a bed for over three months.

In one corner of the clinic the daily activity of a tall young Ethiopian was testimony to the truth that refugees are survivors. Each day the young man pounded away on an old typewriter. He wanted to learn to type, because he knew that skill would help him find a job. He had once been the headmaster of a school, but early one morning soldiers arrived, demanding that he deliver to them his students. He refused and was brutally beaten. After pummeling him with the butts of their rifles, the soldiers left him for dead. Teachers arriving later found him still alive. They could not take him for medical care. They concealed him for months and nursed him back to health. He was blind in one eye and half his face was paralyzed but he was alive. Setting out on foot, he finally reached Nairobi. With the help of the International Rescue Committee he was beginning a new life.

In 1977 IRC returned to Zaire, now a country of asylum for more than a half million refugees who had fled from Angola. IRC's

IRC returned to Zaire in 1977 to help Angolans fleeing Marxist oppression. Louis A. Wiesner, administrator of IRC's overseas medical programs (now a board member), went to Zaire to reestablish services.

More than a hundred thousand pounds of food and nutritional supplements were distributed by IRC to the Angolan refugees, along with blankets, soap, and other emergency relief supplies.

primary objective was to provide medical services, food, and nutritional supplements. More than a hundred thousand pounds of rice, beans, fish, powdered milk, and canned foods were distributed the first year IRC was operating. In cooperation with Medecins Sans Frontieres the program was expanded to include an extensive immunization campaign. Louis A. Wiesner, then IRC's overseas program director and now a member of the board of directors, played a key role in developing the program in Zaire.

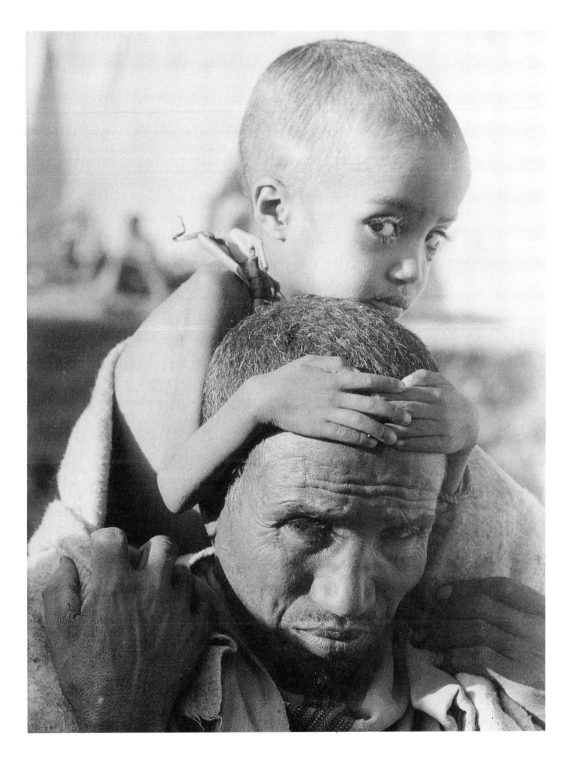

This father and child were among the thousands of Ethiopians who fled to Kenya.

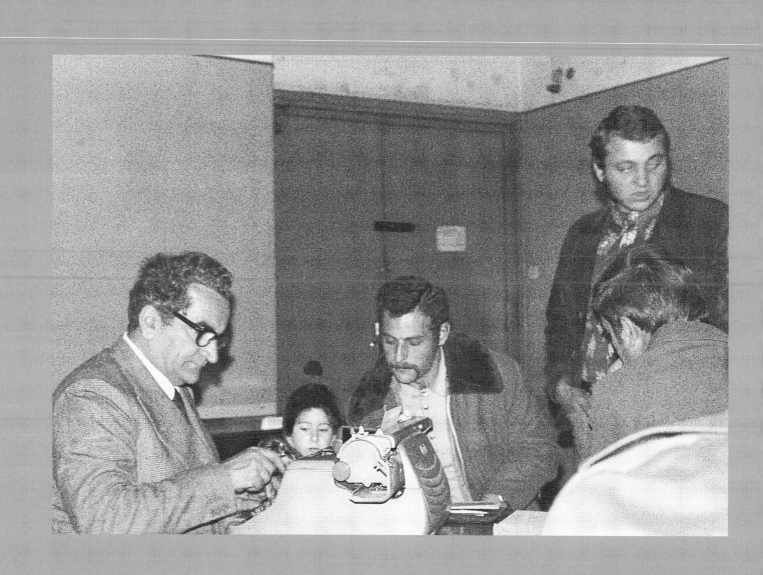

The Desire for Democracy Endures
Behind the Iron Curtain

▶ ▶ ▶ ▶ ▶ ▶ ▶ ▶ ▶ ▶ ▶

Meanwhile, people were on the move in another part of the world, the Soviet Union. Outspoken dissidents, persecuted Jews and Armenians, and many Christians demanded freedom. At the same time, economic problems and pressure from the outside world converged to force open the gates of oppression.

Emigrés, who often waited years to obtain visas, were not allowed to work while they waited and had to leave behind their possessions. Many suffered physical abuse and personal indignities. The majority were Jews, considered by the government to be the most undesirable of the minorities looking outward. Among those coming to the United States and other countries were many writers, artists, and scientists who had suffered persecution and imprisonment because they were Jewish or human rights advocates or both.

A full-time volunteer serving as IRC's vice president for Europe, Garret G. Ackerson, Jr., coordinated the agency's activities from Geneva. With the cooperation of its offices in Rome, Vienna, Munich, Madrid, and Paris, IRC prepared for the new wave of refugees. Ackerson, who had had a long and distinguished career in the foreign service, including serving as U.S. consul general in Budapest at the time of the Hungarian revolution, was well prepared for this task.

The story told by Mihail, a Jewish refugee from Russia, is a story that could have been told by thousands. He was born in the village of Zetl, once in Poland but seized by the Russians in 1939. When Germans attacked his village in 1941, his family fled. His parents and siblings did not survive the Holocaust. For six years Mihail was forced to serve in the Russian army. He was sent to the front because he was a Jew. He survived the war, then moved to Moscow. In 1973 he received his exit visa only after stating that his intention was to go to Israel. A year later he was joined there by his wife. After spending three years on a kibbutz, he and his wife wanted to leave Israel, in part because his wife was not of Jewish origin.

The reasons for wanting to leave one's homeland and venture into the unknown are varied. An IRC caseworker in the Rome office recorded these statements made by Jewish refugees leaving the Soviet Union:

Rade Korach, director of IRC's office in Rome, registered Russian émigrés applying for asylum in the United States.

It was not possible to live in the USSR having an open heart to the spiritual level of life. Most people live only on the material plane and do not imagine that there is anything else to life. Communism takes care of the material needs of the people only, but what about their spiritual needs?

I was never imprisoned. I lived rather well. I had good work in my field, good pay, my own apartment. Yes, I had everything, but I did not leave for material reasons. The USSR is a very big but also very unhappy country. I felt trapped there; but there was no place to go. I only live once. I want to know other cultures, the whole world, other psychologies, art, technology.

I left the USSR for every possible reason there is: material, moral, cultural—everything.

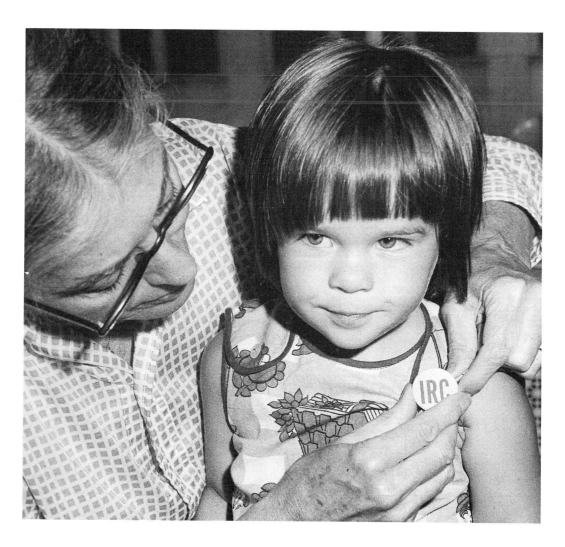

Volunteer Anna Matson in one of IRC's regional centers responsible for the resettlement of Soviet and East European refugees in the United States.

In the United States, many of the Soviet émigrés were helped by IRC to resettle and start new lives.

Throughout the 1970s IRC offices in Europe continued to assist refugees from Czechoslovakia, Hungary, Poland, Bulgaria, Romania, Albania, and Yugoslavia. IRC's efforts were generously supported by the American Council for Judaism Philanthropic Fund, headed by longtime IRC board member Charles Tanenbaum.

Of special concern to IRC were Czechoslovak dissidents, members of the "Charter 77" movement who had signed a manifesto in January 1977 urging the government to respect human rights. In 1980 the Czechoslovak police launched a drive against intellectual and cultural leaders. The dissidents

who reached Austria and eventually other countries were assisted by IRC, and those who chose to resettle in the United States were sponsored by IRC.

In 1945, at the end of World War II, Irma Kadmon Sternberg joined IRC as a caseworker in New York. She retired in 1985 as director of resettlement programs. During her forty years with IRC she enabled thousands of refugees to begin again.

Russian family members reunited at Kennedy Airport after years of separation.

Soviet Invasion Forces
Five Million Afghans into Exile

▷ ▷ ▷ ▷ ▷ ▷ ▷ ▷ ▷ ▷ ▷

In 1986, seven years after Soviet forces rolled into Afghanistan, Edward Giraudet, a correspondent who had covered the war from its beginning, reported:

Migratory genocide remains an essential feature of Soviet strategy, which hinges on large-scale ground offensives, aerial bombardment, and burning of crops. An estimated five million people—that is one out of every three Afghan citizens—have fled from their country since the fighting began.

It was early in 1980, soon after the Soviet invasion, that IRC president John C. Whitehead made the first of his many trips to the Afghanistan-Pakistan border, where hundreds of thousands of Afghans had taken refuge. After witnessing what was happening, he met with government leaders in Pakistan and U. S. officials to lay the groundwork for an ambitious program of emergency assistance.

Entire villages had fled and resettled as communities, so long-standing leadership remained in place. In all his negotiating and planning, Whitehead consulted with the Afghan leaders.

He recalls visiting the makeshift refugee settlements that had begun to crop up in barren northwest Pakistan. There were not yet any camps, only villages where refugees were congregating. Whitehead sat on dusty plots of land where Afghan leaders spread out their rugs to kneel for conversations about what was needed most urgently.

The Afghan refugees, he recalls, were fierce, and all carried guns—usually British Endfields, remnants of World War I. He remembers their gratitude for the food and tents being offered. But what they really wanted, the Afghans made clear, were guns and bullets. They were angry and resentful and they wanted their homeland back.

Whitehead visited remote refugee villages inaccessible by road, because no road existed. Once there, he spoke about United States concern and the help being provided by the International Rescue Committee. When he finished one talk, he was greeted by a young Afghan in traditional garb. Whitehead was startled when the young man declared in perfect English, "That was a heck of a speech." The young man, it turned out, had studied at Harvard Law School and then returned to Kabul, where he had become a local leader.

The flight to Pakistan.

Early in 1980 IRC president John C. Whitehead went to Pakistan to initiate relief, medical, child care, education, and self-help programs for the Afghan refugees.

Half of the refugees in the desolate camps of Pakistan were children, and IRC devoted special attention to alleviating their suffering.

By the end of 1980 IRC was operating an extensive program of relief for the swelling number of refugees that would soon reach three million. IRC's first priority was medical assistance. Mobile clinics were organized and dispensary tents were set up. Scouts went into the scattered encampments to bring sick refugees to the medical tents. Education programs for the children began almost immediately. Soon an extensive network of medical, public health, child care, feeding, educational, training, and self-help programs had been developed. IRC's work focused on the needs of women and children, who made up more than 75 percent of the Afghan refugee population.

No one knew when the Afghans might be able to return to their homeland. Each year saw more and more refugees fleeing to Pakistan. In a single month of 1981 alone, thirty-eight thousand patients were treated at an IRC clinic. Almost half were children under the age of twelve. IRC increasingly concentrated its resources on public health

IRC's medical and public health services for the homeless Afghans included mobile health units, hospitals, dispensaries, mother-and-child centers, sanitation projects, disease control, and special feeding programs for malnourished children. Afghan and Pakistani doctors and nurses were recruited for the massive effort, and additional refugees were trained to serve as medical aides.

A high school for Afghan girls—the only one in Pakistan—was established by IRC in Peshawar. Other IRC work for refugee women included the establishment of a hospital specializing in obstetrics and gynecology and the development of handicrafts projects to help women produce and market their products.

OPPOSITE:

Hundreds of schools were supported and staffed by IRC in Pakistani camps to enable young people to continue their education.

programs and education and heightened its emphasis on preventive medicine.

By 1984 IRC's humanitarian work for Afghan refugees included mobile medical teams; medical dispensaries where refugees were not only treated but also educated about good health practices; maternal-child health units providing pre- and postnatal care; an extensive vaccination program for children; intensive training programs in community health and sanitation; and a special clinic for gynecological care, obstetrics, and pediatrics. To cope with pervasive problems of malnutrition and high mortality rates, IRC combined supplemental feeding for children with nutrition education for mothers.

As the war dragged on, years in confinement led to the growing urgency for more educational programs. "We have lost an entire generation of our children to illiteracy," lamented one Afghan mother. IRC's

work ranged from preschool education to postgraduate courses. The training enabled uprooted Afghans to pursue their aspirations while preparing them for the day when they might return home and rebuild their country. A special high school for refugee girls in Peshawar offered courses in the arts, the sciences, religion, and English.

Advanced learning programs for adults included literacy, English-language training, public administration and management courses, computer training, journalism, a special school of the sciences, and a construction engineering program.

The principle of helping refugees build for the future was also carried out through a network of income-generating projects. Vocational training and employment were provided in fields such as construction and metal working, handicrafts and small-business enterprises, and agriculture and reforestation.

SOVIET INVASION FORCES FIVE MILLION AFGHANS INTO EXILE

A network of self-reliance programs that helped thousands of Afghan families to become self-supporting was developed by IRC. Machine work and textile production, farming and fruit tree cultivation, irrigation and reforestation were among the programs. A large-scale printing operation that employed hundreds of refugees provided camps and schools with books and other educational materials.

An IRC printing workshop that trained hundreds of refugees provided textbooks and other educational materials for refugee camps and schools. This project supported itself through sales.

Special programs for women, such as the high school in Peshawar, were challenged by some radical fundamentalists. At times, threats of bombings and bodily harm forced IRC to suspend these projects. Yet IRC never wavered in its commitment to improving the lives of Afghan women, who have become a driving force in the displaced refugee community in Pakistan. They will play critical roles in education, health care, management, and business when they return to their homeland.

IRC conducted an agriculture survey of areas of rural Afghanistan, land destroyed or left uncultivated for years. Cross-border teams were organized to repair roads, rebuild farms, put irrigation systems back into place, and establish public health and sanitation facilities. A major impediment to repatriation are the land mines—as many as thirty million—scattered across the landscape. IRC has trained thousands of refugees in mine awareness.

In 1988 a Citizens Commission on Afghan Refugees headed by IRC board member Lionel Olmer was formed to study the staggering issues confronting the refugees who would return home once Soviet forces withdrew. Humanitarian, social, economic, logistical, and political problems were evaluated. The commission's recommendations were important not only to IRC but also to other voluntary agencies and governmental organizations planning for the future of Afghanistan.

Palestinian Refugees Receive Assistance

▶ ▶ ▶ ▶ ▶ ▶ ▶ ▶ ▶ ▶ ▶

The International Rescue Committee began a relief and medical program in Lebanon in 1982. The work began in war-stricken Beirut but soon expanded to Sidon, where an Intermediate Health Care Unit (IHCU) was set up to provide diagnostic and therapeutic services for Palestinian refugees as well as Lebanese displaced by the fighting. Dr. Daniel Weiner of the IRC board played a critical role in establishing this unit. In 1984 alone, more than eighteen thousand patients were treated, half of them children, at this IRC facility. An outreach program enabled nurses recruited by IRC to make home visits to outlying areas. IRC staff worked closely with local agencies and the Lebanese Red Cross.

As violence around Sidon escalated, the U.S. State Department pressed IRC to leave. IRC continued to train and support indigenous staff, knowing that it might soon be forced to withdraw from the region. In December 1985 the Commissioner General of the United Nations Relief and Works Agency for Palestinian Refugees (UNRWA) in Geneva sent a letter to IRC that read:

> Your dedicated staff quickly established an enviable reputation. This was occasioned by two major factors—the complementary timing of the IHCU operation to cover times when UNRWA health centers are closed. Further, the staff extended knowledge and competence of our health staff by imaginative in-service education programs. I am informed that administrative cooperation between your Committee and this Agency has been of the highest order.

Finally forced to withdraw, IRC turned over to local personnel the programs it had established.

OPPOSITE AND LEFT:

Emergency relief work by IRC in war-devastated Beirut included rebuilding Palestinian as well as Lebanese refugees' homes. IRC also supported an emergency trauma unit at the American University Hospital in Beirut.

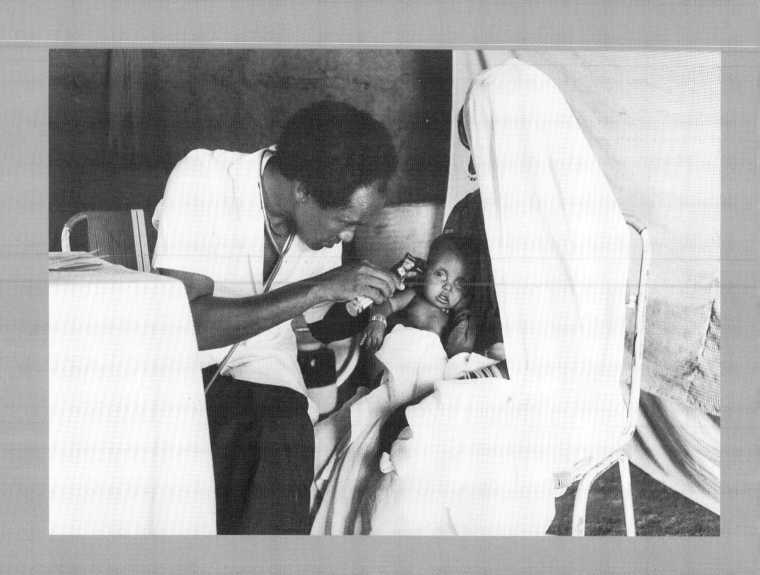

Persecution and Famine Engulf Africa

▶ ▶ ▶ ▶ ▶ ▶ ▶ ▶ ▶ ▶

Throughout the 1980s the African continent erupted in violence again and again. Waves of refugees were forced to flee. Severe famine added to the adversity.

One of the hardest hit countries was Ethiopia. A stream of refugees headed toward Sudan. In 1980 IRC initiated medical and health care programs there and offered training for the displaced.

In 1981 IRC board member Bayard Rustin went to Sudan and Somalia, where desperate Ethiopians were seeking safety and help. His report urged substantial assistance for the hundreds of thousands of refugees.

That same year IRC president John Whitehead visited Somalia. Shortly thereafter IRC initiated a medical program for the Ethiopian refugees. IRC established itself at two camps in the Gedo region, a remote, desolate area with the hottest climate in all of Africa. IRC's work included health clinics, pharmaceutical dispensaries, a tuberculosis center, feeding stations for malnourished children, immunization campaigns, and obstetrical services. An extensive network of community health workers was trained, and more than fifty Somali doctors and nurses were recruited for the program. Within a short period IRC was able to turn over the projects to indigenous staff.

In the winter of 1984 a massive exodus to Sudan was taking place out of the Ethiopian provinces of Tigre and Eritrea, where independence movements were clashing with Ethiopia's Marxist government. Within a year two thousand IRC-trained refugees were providing medical and public health services to nearly five hundred thousand uprooted Ethiopians. The work soon expanded to include child care and emergency feeding programs as well. IRC's program in Sudan was highly praised by the United Nations High Commissioner for Refugees: "IRC's refugee staff is a unique feature of the Sudan program. IRC enables them to serve their own countrymen, thus following the philosophy of helping refugees to help themselves."

In 1985 the crisis intensified in Sudan as the exodus of starving Ethiopians grew. IRC accelerated its efforts. Soon its staff numbered sixty-three expatriate doctors, nurses, nurse practitioners, public health professionals, nutrition experts, and child care specialists. More than five hundred refugees were trained to help staff the programs.

Conditions in Sudan were extreme, with temperatures reaching 120 degrees. Despite severe conditions, dramatic gains were made. When IRC began working in Sudan, the daily mortality rate among the refugees was twenty-five per ten thousand—deaths caused primarily

In 1980 IRC sent medical personnel to Sudan to serve sick and starving refugees fleeing famine and political oppression in Ethiopia.

Teaching Ethiopian refugees to make wood-conserving cookstoves was one of IRC's self-help projects.

In the winter of 1984 a vast new wave of Ethiopians began crossing the border into Sudan. IRC dispatched additional teams of doctors and nurses to the camps, and within a year more than two thousand of the refugees had been trained to help IRC provide medical, public health, child care, and emergency feeding services to five hundred thousand Ethiopian refugees.

by malnutrition. Soon the rate was reduced to three per ten thousand, and a few months later to one.

Another refugee emergency erupted in 1987, when more than four hundred thousand victims of the brutal civil war ravaging Mozambique fled to neighboring Malawi. IRC rushed doctors and nurses to this small country of refuge to treat the women and children, especially the wounded and the starving. As the numbers of Mozambicans

seeking safety in Malawi continued to swell, IRC expanded its efforts to include public and community health education, water and sanitation projects, immunization campaigns, and feeding centers for children.

Few refugee camps emerged because the people of Malawi welcomed the refugees and integrated them into their towns and villages. In close cooperation with the Malawi Ministry of Health, IRC programs benefited not only the Mozambican refugees but the people

IRC taught Mozambican refugee women the basics of nutrition and disease prevention and trained them to become community health workers.

FLIGHT

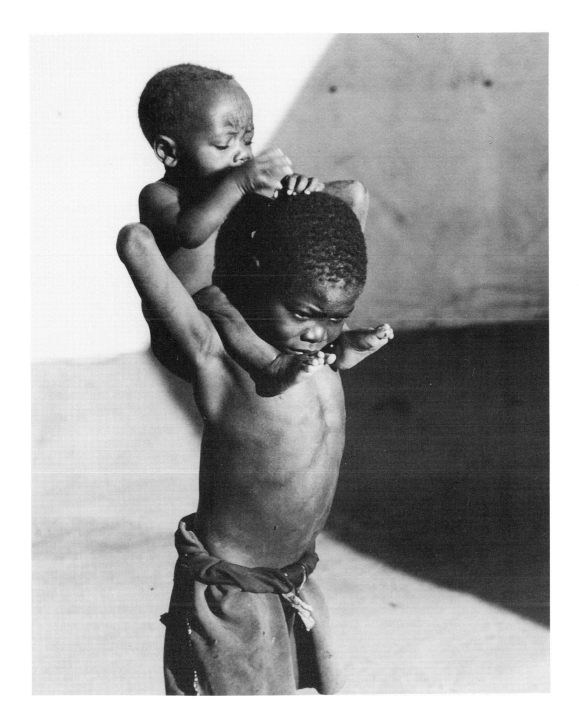

Most of the refugees who escaped to Malawi from the violent civil war sweeping Mozambique were children. IRC medical teams helped restore their health, enabling them to survive.

of Malawi as well. The network of health workers proved critical when a 1989 cholera outbreak threatened many communities. An emergency training session was held. IRC-trained community health workers helped avert an epidemic.

WOMEN'S COMMISSION FOR REFUGEE WOMEN AND CHILDREN

The Women's Commission for Refugee Women and Children was founded in 1989 by IRC board members Catherine O'Neill and Liv Ullmann, and Susan Forbes Martin, the executive director of the Commission on Immigration Reform. The purpose of the commission is to call attention to the particular plight of women and children refugees, and to advocate their cause.

Delegations of volunteer board members conduct site visits to refugee-impacted regions of the world. Follow-up includes written reports with specific recommendations, testimony before Congressional leadership, and working with the media to call attention to issues of concern. An ongoing breakfast series, organized in cooperation with the Lawyers Committee for Human Rights, provides a forum for the discussion of refugee and humanitarian issues. Commission members also make presentations to various civic groups, schools, and conferences. In 1992 the commission sponsored an international symposium on repatriation. As part of its ongoing public education efforts the commission completed and distributed a video entitled Voices *that includes footage from delegation visits.*

Since its inception the Women's Commission has visited Somalia, Ethiopia, Malawi, Mozambique, Liberia, Guinea, Ivory Coast, Pakistan, Laos, Cambodia, Vietnam, Thailand, El Salvador, Nicaragua, Guatemala, Mexico, Haiti, Bosnia, and Croatia.

The Women's Commission strongly advocates that the international community and relief agencies give greater attention to responding to violence against refugee women. Plans are under way to establish a trauma hostel for Bosnian women and to replicate its most effective aspects in other regions. Other priorities include: improving birth-spacing options for refugee women; advocating earlier intervention into humanitarian crises; focusing attention on areas of suffering not highlighted by the media; and pressing for United Nations' guidelines for the treatment of refugee women and children.

At one of the Women's Commission annual luncheons Liv Ullmann spoke to a roomful of people asking the question, What can I do? She replied: "We can bring the faces and stories to the headlines and to the classrooms and to those who make decisions. Educating our own communities and our children may be the most important thing we do in life."

▷ ▷ ▷ ▷

Catherine O'Neill, cofounder of the commission, on one of many missions.

In January 1990 a delegation led by Liv Ullmann, a cofounder of the Women's Commission for Refugee Women and Children, inspected the Hong Kong detention camps for Vietnamese refugees. The commission's report strongly focused on the plight and urgent needs of the children, and on their precarious health in particular.

Crises in Cuba and
Central America Uproot Thousands

▶ ▶ ▶ ▶ ▶ ▶ ▶ ▶ ▶ ▶

Events in Latin America called for IRC's best efforts. In 1980 discontent in Havana drove hundreds of Cubans into the Swiss embassy, where they sought safety and exit visas. Castro at first agreed to allow them to leave. Soon seafaring craft of all kind were headed for Mariel, a port where the Cubans were to be picked up. At the peak of the activity more than thirteen hundred boats were in the harbor, with families awaiting the arrival of their relatives still inside the embassy.

Then, Castro changed his mind. The rescue boats were denied permission to depart. This was a startling setback. Many of those on the boats had sacrificed most everything to finance the trip to Mariel.

Finally it was announced that the boats would have to leave without the family members they had come to rescue. Castro forced back into Havana many of those who were crowded into the embassy. He chose instead to expel hundreds of Cubans he considered undesirable—criminals, petty thieves, and homosexuals. Castro knew that these refugees would not be so welcome in the United States, yet he realized that the United States government could not refuse to admit the exiled Cubans. This scenario points to the complexity of refugee issues: IRC helped in resettling some of those admitted, but serious criminal offenders were deported from the United States.

In the fall of 1983 IRC collaborated with local medical organizations in the Chiapas province of southern Mexico, where more than forty-five thousand Guatemalans had fled. The refugees were mostly Indian peasants, half of them children, who benefited from a pediatric unit established at a local hospital. It was the only such facility providing services for the refugees.

In 1984 IRC responded to the civil war in El Salvador, where more than five hundred thousand people were uprooted by bloody fighting. Medical programs, public health education, and self-help projects were established. IRC's clinic, mother-child centers, and nutritional units reached out to over fifty refugee communities. Vaccination coverage reached 90 percent of the villages. Training in nutrition, midwifery, environmental sanitation, literacy, home gardening, and animal husbandry was provided.

Salvadorans who desired to integrate permanently in areas where they had taken refuge were helped with constructing housing and rehabilitating community infrastructure such as water and

Between April and September 1980 a freedom flotilla of more than 1,200 boats brought 125,000 refugees from Cuba to the United States. Thousands of those who escaped were resettled by IRC.

In El Salvador, ravaged by civil war, IRC's medical, health, and feeding programs devoted special attention to uprooted mothers and children.

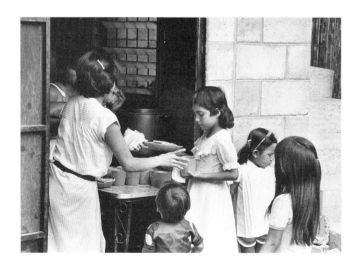

sewage systems, roads, schools and meeting houses, and agriculture. Education and training was critical in all the programs, helping to create new self-sustaining communities.

During this same period more than twenty-five thousand Miskito Indians were forced to flee persecution in Nicaragua. IRC responded after a visit by executive director Carel Sternberg. A public health nurse was dispatched to Honduras, where the refugees had fled. In January 1984 an article entitled "The Tragedy of the Miskito Indians" was published in the French newspaper *Le Matin*. The author was IRC board member Elie Wiesel, who had visited the areas where refugees had gathered. The article included these words:

> Somewhere in the Honduran jungle, along the Mocoron River, the people of an old, traditionally peaceful and hardworking Indian tribe called the Miskitos are trying to rebuild their homes and their dreams. Not far from there, on the other side of the Nicaraguan border, a

IRC self-help projects in Salvadoran refugee communities included agricultural and gardening projects and house construction. These efforts were consistent with IRC's long-range goal to help displaced Salvadorans wishing to integrate permanently where they had taken refuge.

regime steeped in violence has tried to change and even destroy their homes and their dreams. Their only desires were to work their lands, swim in their river, speak their own language, gather in the Moravian churches, listen to the secret sounds of the forest, celebrate holidays and weddings.

The Sandinistas, wishing to strengthen their borders, expelled the Miskitos from their villages, declaring the sites "military zones." Faced with the refusal of the Indians, soldiers began to burn houses and kill livestock. Other cruelties followed: arrests, humiliations, executions.

Some twenty-five thousand Miskito Indians persecuted by the Sandinista government of Nicaragua found asylum in Honduras. IRC compensated for the absence of schools by organizing an education-by-radio program.

In 1985 IRC organized an education-by-radio program that reached more than forty remote villages in Honduras, where the Miskitos had settled. Refugees were trained to serve as monitor-teachers in their camps and were provided with radio receivers, paper and pencils, and blackboards. Not only the children learned, but so did adults. In 1988 IRC was able to turn over the program to local Hondurans and Miskito refugees.

This wall of case folders for Spanish refugees is indicative of the massive numbers of people who fled to France during the Spanish Civil War and Francisco Franco's dictatorship. Surviving refugees and family members in France are still helped today by Spanish Refugee Aid, a division of the IRC.

SERVING REFUGEES FROM
SPANISH CIVIL WAR CONTINUES

In 1984 Spanish Refugee Aid (SRA) became a self-supporting member of the IRC family. SRA had been established in 1953 to assist refugees who had fled to France from the civil war that had ravaged Spain during the 1930s. Thousands of exiles and their families were helped through medical relief services. From a small office in Toulouse, France, caseworkers provided direct assistance to refugees, many quite elderly, as well as scholarships for their children. SRA is a continuation of the work IRC carried out in France during and after the Spanish civil war decades ago.

▶ ▶ ▶ ▶

IRC Supports Solidarność Inside Poland

▶ ▶ ▶ ▶ ▶ ▶ ▶ ▶ ▶ ▶

As the Solidarity movement swept Poland in the early 1980s and the danger of Soviet intervention heightened, a growing number of Poles sought asylum. Within days after the military takeover on December 13, 1981, Leo Cherne flew to Austria to lay the groundwork for a relief and resettlement effort. IRC aided several hundred Poles in obtaining refugee status and helped many resettle in the United States, Canada, and Australia.

IRC's involvement in Poland intensified again in October 1987, when it initiated a medical assistance program funded by the National Endowment for Democracy. The work was carried out in partnership with the Polish trade union movement, Solidarność, headed by Lech Walesa. Solidarność was struggling for a free and democratic government for Poland.

A committee comprising American doctors of Polish descent, members of the IRC board of directors, and representatives of the AFL-CIO was organized to oversee the program. Diagnostic centers, independent of the state health service, were established in three industrial cities. A network of centers for mammographic screening was also set up. Ambulances as well as diagnostic equipment provided by American and other Western-based corporations were delivered to Poland. Volunteer doctors offered demonstrations on the equipment and lectured to hospital staffs in Warsaw, Legnica, and Gdańsk.

When a freely elected government was installed in Poland, at last replacing the one-party Communist regime that had ruled the country for more than forty years, Lech Walesa became its president.

OPPOSITE:

A room at the Traiskirchen camp in Austria: following the military take-over of Poland in 1981, waves of refugees fled to free West European countries. IRC offices in Vienna, Munich, Rome, and Paris assisted thousands of Polish escapees. Many of them were resettled by IRC in the United States—in April 1982 alone, 170 Polish refugees were received at IRC's New York office.

LEFT:

United States ambassador to Poland, John Davis (second from left), welcomes the first of three fully equipped ambulances that were part of the extensive IRC-sponsored program inside Poland.

Kurdish Refugee Emergency Leads to New Responses

▶ ▶ ▶ ▶ ▶ ▶ ▶ ▶ ▶ ▶

The needs of the world's refugees far exceed available resources. Refugee emergencies arise with little warning and in unexpected places. These crises are complex and resolutions are difficult to realize.

In the early days of the Persian Gulf War, IRC operations director Roy Williams, along with board members Julia Taft and Lionel Rosenblatt, set up emergency relief programs for the nearly one million "guest workers" from Asian and African countries forced out of Kuwait and Iraq into Jordan. Upon their arrival the delegation received this note from the Crown Prince of Jordan:

> I was gratified to learn that you and your colleagues of the International Rescue Committee have already taken steps to translate your commitment to the high humanitarian ideals into practical measure, aiming at providing relief to the tens of thousands of workers who are, or may be, passing through Jordan.

The refugees huddled in hastily erected desert camps near the Iraqi border, where temperatures reached 120 degrees during the day and plummeted to below 40 at night. Such harsh extremes exacerbated an already difficult situation.

IRC launched a public health and sanitation program in two of the largest refugee camps in Jordan. Latrines were constructed, drainage systems were improved, refuse disposal systems were put into place, water usage was monitored, roads were surveyed and resurfaced, and temporary housing was constructed. By December 1990 only forty-five hundred refugees remained in the camps. The others had returned to their homelands without loss of life from disease.

The tragedy of the Kurdish refugees that erupted following the Persian Gulf War bears witness to the need to respond to such emergencies without delay. Starting in April 1991 hundreds of thousands of Kurds fleeing Saddam Hussein's terror and persecution were driven into the mountains along the Iraq-Turkey border. They had nowhere else to go and no one to turn to for help. Huddled together in the snow and rain were children, women, and men struggling to survive. IRC responded immediately.

Board members James Strickler, Julia Taft, and Lionel Olmer were dispatched. En route to Iraq they were briefed by the U.S. ambassador to Turkey, Morton Abramowitz, who later

Saddam Hussein's campaign of terror drove hundreds of thousands of Kurdish refugees into the mountainous area along the Iraq-Turkey border. IRC relief and medical teams were rushed to the scene to help the refugees survive.

Almost a million Asian and African "guest workers" fled Iraq and Kuwait to Jordan following the 1990 invasion of Kuwait by Saddam Hussein's military forces. IRC emergency teams provided sanitation services and temporary housing for refugees packed into desert camps.

Most of the Kurdish refugees were women and children.

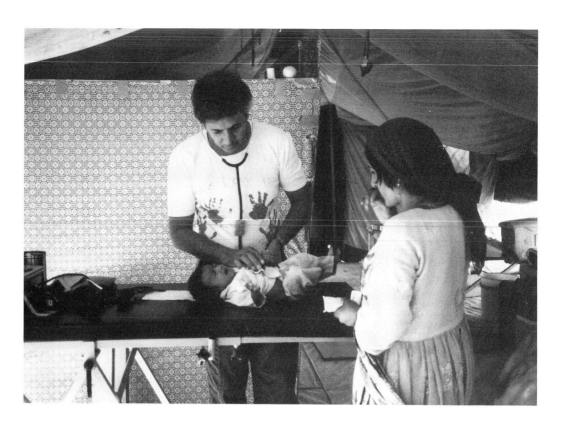

The babies among the Kurdish refugees required special care from IRC doctors and nurses.

became a member of the IRC board of directors. His wife, Sheppie, is IRC's Washington representative.

Work began: clean water sources were identified and protected, latrines were built, and emergency shelter was constructed. Refugees were trained to assist with emergency health measures and community education. Delegation members who had returned to the United States began raising awareness about the plight of the Kurds. IRC was instrumental in moving the Bush administration toward a decision to deploy military resources to the refugee crisis.

The Kurds, aided and reassured by the presence of allied military forces, began coming down out of the mountains to return to secured sites inside Iraq. IRC set up medical screening points along the routes of return and worked with other voluntary agencies and the coalition forces to establish public health, medical, and sanitation programs in refugee camps.

As the Kurds returned to their villages, IRC assisted with the immense task of rebuilding. The immediate need was shelter, so IRC began a construction program. Medical facilities were rehabilitated, and water and sanitation systems were repaired. Agricultural assistance was also provided; seeds and tools were distributed.

THE LEO CHERNE REFUGEE EMERGENCY FUND

IRC realized emergencies such as the Kurdish refugee crisis would occur again and again. Clearly the "immediate response" fund that Leo Cherne had been pressing for for years was needed. When he stepped down in August 1991 after serving as IRC chairman for forty years, the IRC board of directors established a refugee emergency fund in Leo's honor.

The initial $1 million goal of the Leo Cherne Refugee Emergency Fund has been realized. Within a little more than a year the fund was drawn upon three times: to begin relief efforts in Somalia; to dispatch an experienced staff person to northern Kenya to define a project for Somali, Sudanese, and Ethiopian refugees; and to initiate sanitation programs in Bangladesh, where nearly three hundred thousand Rohingya refugees had fled to escape oppression in Burma.

▷ ▷ ▷ ▷

Violence in Former Yugoslavia Threatens World Stability

▶ ▶ ▶ ▶ ▶ ▶ ▶ ▶ ▶ ▶

The 1990s are presenting unprecedented challenges to the International Rescue Committee. As the crises in former Yugoslavia and Somalia mounted, new ways of responding to complex crises were needed.

Once the enemies of IRC's efforts were dysentery and malaria. Now the enemy carries a gun. Relief workers must confront not only the problems of poor sanitation and too few supplies but also the threat of warlords. New times require new responses.

Led by board members John Richardson, Julia Taft, Richard Holbrooke, and Lionel Rosenblatt, the International Rescue Committee has been working in former Yugoslavia since January 1992. Amidst a chaotic and ever-changing situation IRC convoys are crisscrossing the war-torn countryside in an effort to make some difference.

Relief routes have been mapped and distribution systems have been established to ensure that supplies reach as many people as possible. IRC was instrumental in organizing the first flight in and out of Sarajevo, helping to evacuate 350 Jews from that beleaguered city.

An extensive winterization project was mounted in the fall of 1992 as death threatened hundreds of thousands of displaced people deprived of essential food, medicines, and shelter. More than 120 tons of food and clothing, blankets, and other supplies were distributed throughout Bosnia-Herzegovina. The extraordinary personal contribution of Ted Forstmann, senior partner of Forstmann Little in New York City and now a member of the IRC board of directors, and the in-kind donations he obtained from a number of leading American corporations made this project possible.

More than forty factories have been reopened to provide much-needed supplies such as heating and cooking stoves, plastics for temporary shelter, building-repair kits, and clothing and boots. In Sarajevo a multimillion-dollar fuel delivery project is being managed, and IRC is reconstructing the water and natural gas systems of that same city.

One of the worst instruments being used in this bloody campaign is the frightful and systematic rape of women; in Bosnia-Herzegovina a program has been established to support women traumatized by rape and violence. IRC is working with local psychologists and

One of the tragic consequences of the ethnic cleansing carried out in Bosnia-Herzegovina was the forcible separation of people along national and religious lines. These two women— one Catholic, the other Muslim—had been close friends since childhood but were nevertheless sent to different refugee camps when their Bosnian village was evacuated.

During the first days of systematic destruction of Bosnian cities and villages, IRC participated in the United Nations–sponsored evacuation of Jewish and Bosnian refugees.

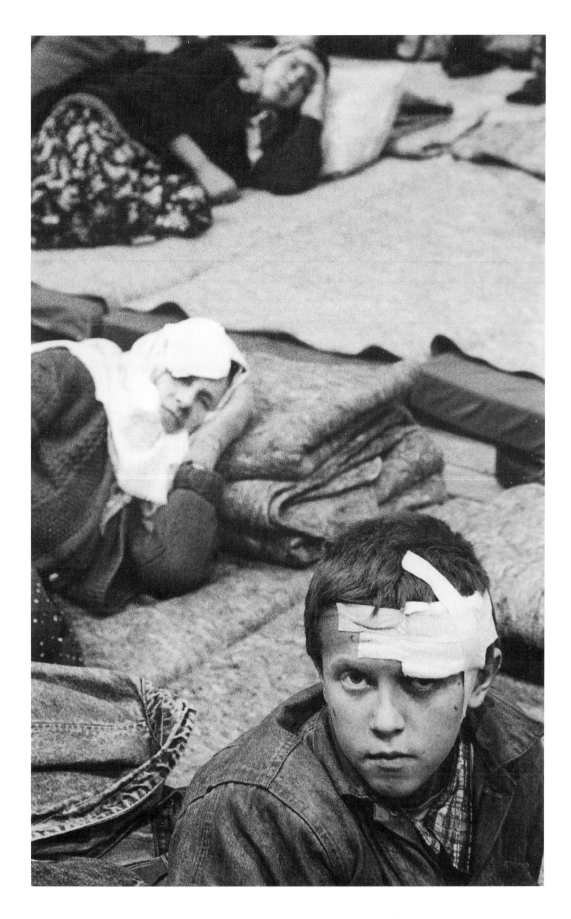

In Mostar and other Bosnian villages, IRC provided emergency shelter for refugees whose homes had been destroyed by shelling and military assaults.

Furnaces and stoves for Bosnian homes were manufactured by IRC-supervised teams in factories that were once used to produce armaments.

counselors to begin what will be a long healing process for these women as well as for the children who have witnessed brutal atrocities. Mental and public health services are also being offered in refugee camps in Croatia.

There is no end in sight to the violence ravaging what was once Yugoslavia. Hundreds of thousands are without homes and other basic needs. There is little hope that they will ever be able to return home. What was once home now belongs to someone else—someone with more rage and a bigger gun.

The ethnic cleansing that has given rise to this appalling violence is a new phenomenon confronting IRC and other international relief agencies. Its horrors are reminiscent of

IRC established special trauma centers for Bosnian women and children who had been subjected to rape and violence.

Mourning the loss of loved ones is a daily scene throughout war-torn Bosnia-Herzegovina.

the agency's early days in Hitler's Europe. Its terror will likely not be confined to former Yugoslavia.

While it continues to save lives and protect the vulnerable in former Yugoslavia, the International Rescue Committee is also pressing for other kinds of action in the international effort to bring this bloody battle to an end. The violence must cease. And the long struggle of rebuilding families and communities and nations must begin.

Albanians crowded into temporary quarters.

ALBANIANS, TOO, ARE FORCED TO ESCAPE OPPRESSION

In July 1990 thousands of Albanians responded to continuing oppression in their country by taking flight. Most of them managed to reach Italy, where IRC dispatched a caseworker to assist with registering the refugees eligible for resettlement abroad. During 1991 more than thirteen hundred Albanians joined family members already living in the United States. IRC helped resettle many of these refugees.

▶ ▶ ▶ ▶

IRC Helps Former Dissidents in Moscow

▷ ▷ ▷ ▷ ▷ ▷ ▷ ▷ ▷ ▷

In 1991 IRC began a program in Moscow, supporting a team of volunteer physicians helping former prisoners of the gulag, freedom fighters who endured much because of their tenacious dedication to liberty. The idea originated with former IRC president William vanden Heuval and was immediately endorsed by Leo Cherne, John Whitehead, Carel Sternberg, and John Richardson. IRC felt a responsibility to assist these individuals who gave so much in their fight for freedom. They paid a heavy price for their political beliefs, losing most everything, including their families. They are broken, alone, and in need of special care. Many of these former dissidents are now elderly, and the majority were physically and psychologically brutalized during their internment. Their medical needs are extreme. A small group of Russian doctors and nurses mounted an effort called the Compassion program to help these former dissidents. Medical care is provided through home visits in and around Moscow, and a wing for inpatient care at a suburban hospital is being managed. IRC is providing drugs, medical equipment, a van, technical oversight, and expertise, as well as small stipends for the nurses and doctors.

Drs. James Strickler and Daniel Weiner have been instrumental in establishing this program. IRC's administrator-consultant for the Moscow medical assistance program was William Buell, who played a similar role with IRC's medical program in Poland. In 1991 IRC ended its formal relationship with the Solidarity Social Foundation, confident that the clinics it had established could continue making significant contributions to the quality of life in Poland.

Linda Pell, director of IRC's Munich office, arranged for a medical van that was driven to Moscow for use by the Compassion program.

Atrocities in Africa Demand
Best Efforts of World Community

▷ ▷ ▷ ▷ ▷ ▷ ▷ ▷ ▷ ▷

When the United Nations High Commissioner for Refugees, Mrs. Sadako Ogata, announced that an emergency relief program for Somalis had to be established, she turned to the International Rescue Committee because of its experience and ability to act fast. Hundreds of thousands of Somalis, uprooted and displaced by civil war and famine, were huddled along the Kenya border in desperate need of help.

IRC quickly organized a cross-border program, providing medical and public health assistance, immunization campaigns and mobile health clinics, water and sanitation projects, and agricultural and veterinary services to more than three hundred thousand victims of violence and drought. Until IRC arrived at Bardera, inside Somalia, there was no sanitation program in place.

Somali refugees in Kenya are also being assisted, along with Ethiopian and Sudanese refugees who have fled to that country. IRC manages public health services and training, immunization programs and mobile health clinics, sanitation projects, and feeding centers. Outreach projects recruit and train refugee community health workers and traditional birth attendants, and the rehabilitation of a regional hospital is underway. Health care workers are assigned to specific families, visiting them on a routine basis to identify problems, monitor improvements, and offer education about preventive measures.

Several of IRC's domestic offices are actively involved in helping Somalis resettle in the United States. Somalis are among the many groups changing the complexion of IRC's resettlement caseload. The staff's experience shows itself in many ways. For example, the director of IRC's San Diego office was invited to Camp Pendleton to prepare U.S. Marines for their tour in Somalia. She helped educate them about customs of the country and taught them phrases in the Somali language.

IRC is occupied in many other regions of Africa. Liberian refugees forced out of their homeland by civil war are being assisted in Ghana, Ivory Coast, and Guinea. In Ghana and Ivory Coast IRC is cooperating with UNIFEM (the U.N.'s development fund for women) in an effort to meet the particular needs of refugee women. Mental health counseling, health education with an emphasis on sexually transmitted diseases, and microbusiness training are

Metal containers were a cherished possessions of Somali refugee children. Without these vessels, there was no hope of obtaining whatever water or food might become available.

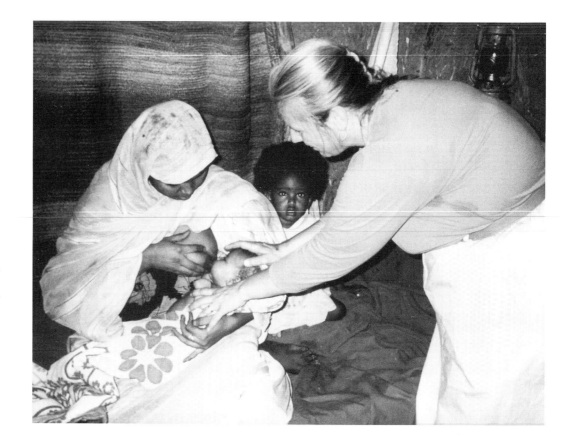

RIGHT AND OPPOSITE:

Somali victims of war and drought were helped in their own country and across the border in Kenya by a variety of IRC medical, sanitation, and child care programs.

BELOW:

Special public health messages were spread to refugees through songs, in keeping with the oral tradition of the Malawi people.

Women and children were the majority of refugees who fled to Guinea from Liberia. IRC developed special programs to meet the needs of the women uprooted by the civil war sweeping their country.

FLIGHT

A refugee settlement in Malawi for Mozambicans seeking asylum.

Refugees lined up daily for basic food supplies provided by IRC. Even the children helped, collecting kernels of corn dropped in the fields.

For the forty thousand Liberian children in Guinea, IRC supported a hundred refugee schools.

all being provided for the women, to help them adjust to a new social and economic situation.

In Guinea IRC administers a hundred refugee schools serving forty thousand primary and secondary students. IRC is providing stipends for teachers, books, and other educational materials and assisting with the development of curricula and exams. Health education is incorporated into the daily teaching, benefiting not only the students but their families and communities. Soon vocational training will begin.

IRC's ongoing programs in four districts of Malawi include training and supervising Mozambican refugee community health workers; community education about hygiene, nutrition, and immunization; latrine construction and waste management; provision of clean water, water testing, well construction, and pump maintenance; providing education materials for schools and helping repair school facilities; supplementary feeding centers that incorporate nutrition education for mothers; and kitchen garden projects.

In southern Sudan IRC medical teams provided emergency medical assistance for the young victims of civil war, starvation, and disease.

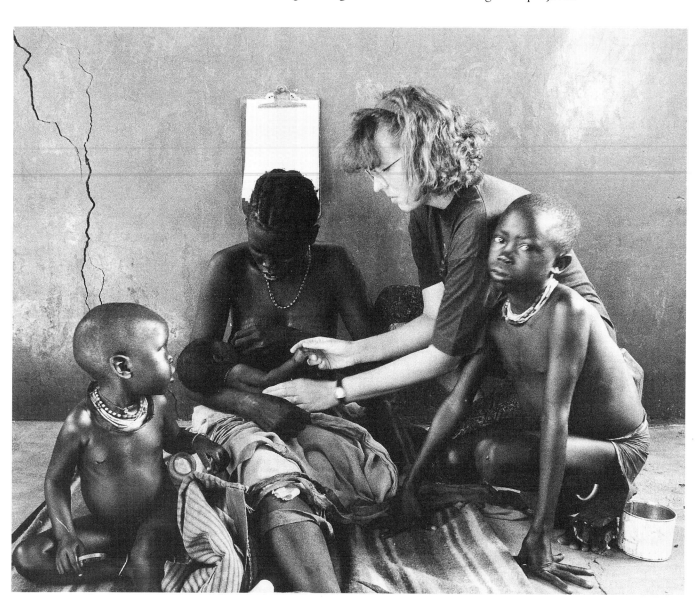

In response to a severe regional drought impacting Malawi in 1992, IRC began a food distribution and nutrition monitoring program. Water and sanitation projects were expanded to reduce the effects of a poor harvest and water scarcity. IRC is now exploring the possibility of refugees repatriating to certain regions of Mozambique.

There were major changes during the early 1990s in eastern Sudan, where IRC has been providing services for Ethiopian refugees since 1980. Public health and curative programs developed by IRC are now being managed entirely by local staff; successful training of refugees led to the withdrawal of IRC's expatriate staff. IRC continues to offer technical assistance, resources, and medicine to help sustain the programs. IRC's presence in eastern Sudan will end as the refugees prepare to repatriate to Ethiopia and to now-independent Eritrea. The extensive skills and training provided by IRC will go with the refugees as they return home.

Gains Are Made in Central America

▶ ▶ ▶ ▶ ▶ ▶ ▶ ▶ ▶ ▶

The establishment of a freely elected government in Nicaragua in 1990 led to the return of refugees who had previously fled to Costa Rica. The Costa Rican government agreed to allow those who wished to stay to remain, and IRC assisted them with permanent resettlement. But for those now able to go home, IRC's role has shifted from refugee relief to repatriation and integration efforts. In Nicaragua IRC began reconstruction and rehabilitation projects in communities receiving returnees.

In El Salvador IRC has been providing community services for thousands of displaced families since 1984. With help from IRC board members Norton Stevens and Angier Duke, a local organization called the Committee for Integration and Reconstruction of El Salvador was formed and by 1992 was fully independent. IRC turned over its responsibilities to this indigenous organization.

IRC is also working in Belize, where more than forty thousand refugees from other Central American countries are living in spontaneous resettlements. Water systems have been installed, and roads and bridges are being constructed. Materials for schools and vocational training centers are being provided. A cattle production project was begun, and seeds and tools are being supplied.

OPPOSITE:

Carpentry and machine work were among the self-help projects sponsored by IRC during the 1980s for Nicaraguan refugees who fled to Costa Rica.

LEFT:

IRC helped Nicaraguans who chose to remain in Costa Rica to build and put down roots.

At Last: Repatriation to Afghanistan

▶ ▶ ▶ ▶ ▶ ▶ ▶ ▶ ▶ ▶ ▶

Thirteen years after it sent emergency medical teams to Pakistan in response to the influx of refugees from Afghanistan, IRC continues to operate extensive refugee programs there. Today IRC activities include medical and educational services, a health education resource center, and self-reliance and income-generating projects. Since 1980 this program has grown into what was, until very recently, IRC's largest program.

Soviet forces have withdrawn and now Afghans are returning home to begin the daunting task of rebuilding their country. IRC remains committed to them during repatriation. A rural assistance project in Afghanistan is increasing productivity and generating income. A rehabilitation project includes repair of irrigation systems, construction of dams and grain warehouses, distribution of seeds and fertilizers, assistance for schools, and public health services. IRC is expanding its cross-border work, anticipating a program that will continue agricultural activities, public health and sanitation services, and education in a new Afghanistan.

Following the withdrawal of Soviet forces in 1990, Afghan refugees in Pakistan started returning home. Inside Afghanistan IRC intensified its repatriation efforts by helping to rebuild the shattered infrastructure.

IRC Advocacy Campaign

▶ ▶ ▶ ▶ ▶ ▶ ▶ ▶ ▶ ▶

Over the past sixty years the International Rescue Committee has served as the public voice of uprooted people unable to speak for themselves. This advocacy role of IRC has endeavored to create worldwide awareness of the needs of refugees and the reasons for their flight—political, religious, and racial oppression, war and famine. It also directly addresses how concerned citizens can help.

A basic component of the advocacy effort has been public service advertising prepared by volunteer agencies and published in magazines and newspapers. The first of the two advertisements shown here, picturing Albert Einstein, goes back many years. The second advertisement was prepared in 1993 by IRC's current volunteer agency, Bozell Worldwide, under the leadership of Jay Schulberg, an IRC board member and chairman of the public affairs committee.

Since 1933, the International Rescue Committee has helped millions of people escaping from the tyranny of political, religious and racial persecution. Today IRC is the leading American nonsectarian refugee organization. Our job is to help people who are literally dying to be free.

We started by helping refugees from Nazi Germany and Mussolini's Italy. That's when Albert Einstein was with us. Now we are helping uprooted Czechs and Hungarians, Cubans and Chileans, Chinese and Albanians, Kurds from Iraq, refugees from the Soviet Union and thousands of Vietnamese, Cambodians and Laotians.

We're fortunate to be living in a country that guarantees our basic freedoms. Consider those who are not. Please help us help them by sending your contributions to: International Rescue Committee, 386 Park Avenue South, New York, N.Y. 10016.

Too bad the I.R.C. isn't as well known as some of the people who have worked with us.

INTERNATIONAL
RESCUE
COMMITTEE
We help people who are dying to be free.

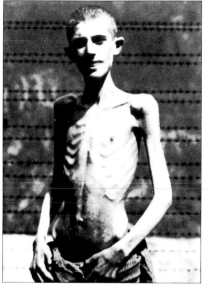

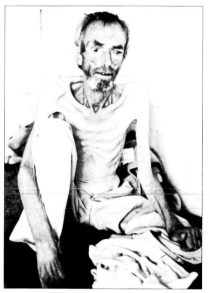

Never forget, 1942.   Never again, 1992.

Have we not learned from the past?

Tragically, history is repeating itself in the atrocities being committed in Bosnia. As world leaders continue to endlessly debate, barbarians mock the civilized world.

The Nazi era has returned: Concentration camps. Starvation. Summary executions. Rape prisons.

Genocide continues unabated:

• A militiaman practices slitting the throats of pigs so he can slit the throats of men.

• 67 people are stuffed into a truck. Inside temperatures soar to 130-140 degrees. 22 suffocate.

• Orphans are killed by snipers.

• A young mother is raped by four soldiers as her baby cries beside her. When she pleads to breast-feed her baby, one rapist cuts off the baby's head.

• Thousands more women are raped. Then murdered.

Millions of refugees.

100,000 people have died. 700,000 are displaced within Bosnia. 2,000,000 more have been driven from their homes. Thousands more will die as a bitter winter sets in.

Does anyone really believe that "ethnic cleansing" will be confined to Bosnia? History teaches us that tyranny unchecked marches on to other lands to commit other atrocities.

Ethnic cleansing will spread. Racial and ethnic hatreds are exploding in Europe and throughout the world as countries disintegrate or as moral authority collapses.

Failure to take strong effective action now sends a signal to the forces of evil that the free world lacks the backbone to stop them.

Timidity in the face of aggression has always failed.

Where are our world leaders? Where are our *own* voices. Where is our soul?

If people and nations had stood up in the 1930's, Nazi barbarianism could have been stopped.

Today, we will be held accountable. By being silent or by being ineffective, we become accomplices.

One day, our children or grandchildren will ask us: When did you know it? What did you *do* about it?

Individually, we are powerless. Collectively, we are strong. There are two things each one of us can do.

One, ask President Bush and President-elect Clinton to:

• Demand that the U.N. Security Council create temporary "safe havens" in Bosnia to protect innocent civilians.

• Provide increased security for humanitarian workers assisting refugees in Bosnia.

• Admit at least 25,000 refugees to the U.S.

• Demand that the U.N. gather evidence of atrocities for future war crimes trials.

• Establish a high level U.N. international commission to assist with reconstruction once the fighting has ceased.

Secondly, we can help the refugees. Those without homes, without food, without hope. The International Rescue Committee can provide shelter, food, medicine, clothing, sanitation and more.

Founded by Albert Einstein.

Founded in 1933 by Albert Einstein to assist refugees who fled Hitler's Germany, the IRC has been helping refugees who escape political, religious and racial persecution ever since.

From the Hungarian Revolution of '56 to Cambodia in '79 to the Kurds in '90 to Somalia today, the IRC has served as a beacon of hope in a sea of indifference and despair.

Please give as generously as you can. Your contribution is tax-deductible.

Send both coupons to the International Rescue Committee. We will forward your views to President Bush and President-elect Clinton.

So someday when your children or grandchildren ask, what did *you* do, you can say you helped save a life. Perhaps, a thousand lives.

To: President Bush and President-elect Clinton.

c/o International Rescue Committee, 386 Park Avenue South, New York, NY 10016

I urge you to take the following actions in the former Yugoslavia:

1. Demand that the U.N. Security Council create temporary "safe havens" in Bosnia to protect innocent civilians.
2. Provide increased security for humanitarian workers assisting refugees in Bosnia.
3. Admit at least 25,000 of the most desperate refugees to the U.S.
4. Demand that the U.N. gather evidence of atrocities for future war crimes trials.
5. Establish a high level U.N. International commission to assist with reconstruction once the fighting has ceased.

Signature _____

Name _____

Address _____

City _____ State _____ Zip _____

To: The International Rescue Committee

Attn: Robert DeVecchi, President, 386 Park Avenue South, New York, NY 10016

I want to make a tax-deductible contribution to the IRC to support the following humanitarian assistance to the refugees in the former Yugoslavia:

1. Provide warm clothing and shelter to protect refugees from the bitter winter.
2. Establish trauma and rape centers for the women.
3. Increase the flow of food and medicine into Bosnia.
4. Provide medical and immunization programs for refugees and displaced persons.
5. Provide clean water sanitation in refugee camps to avoid typhoid and cholera.

Enclosed is my tax-deductible contribution of:

☐ $35   ☐ $50   ☐ $100   ☐ $500   Or $_____

Name _____

Address _____

City _____ State _____ Zip _____

International Rescue Committee
Founded by Albert Einstein in 1933.

This ad paid for by private contributions. You can obtain the latest financial audit from IRC or the Office of Charities Registration, NY Department of State, Albany, NY 12231.

IRC Freedom Awards

▶ ▶ ▶ ▶ ▶ ▶ ▶ ▶ ▶ ▶

The International Rescue Committee first bestowed its Freedom Award for extraordinary contributions to the cause of refugees and human freedom to Willy Brandt. The year was 1957. Most recently, in 1992, the Freedom Award was given to Cyrus Vance, the Secretary General of the United Nations' personal envoy for peace-keeping efforts in former Yugoslavia.

The list of those who have received the Freedom Award reveals the remarkable ability of an individual to shape history and change for the better a world moving toward freedom for all.

1957	WILLY BRANDT
1958	WINSTON CHURCHILL
1959	WILLIAM DONOVAN
1960	RICHARD E. BYRD
1965	GEORGE MEANY
1966	DAVID DUBINSKY
1967	DAVID SARNOFF
1969	LUCIUS D. CLAY
1970	JACOB K. JAVITS
1975	BRUNO KREISKY
1976	LEO CHERNE
1977	HUBERT H. HUMPHREY
1978	JOSEPH BUTTINGER
1979	MARY PILLSBURY LORD (posthumously)
1981	LANE KIRKLAND and IRENA KIRKLAND
1987	ELIE WIESEL
1987	JOHN C. WHITEHEAD
1989	SADRUDDIN AGA KHAN
1989	LECH WALESA
1990	VIOLETTA BARRIOS DE CHAMORRO
1991	FANG LIZHI and LI SHUXIAN
1991	JAVIER PÉREZ DE CUÉLLAR
1992	CYRUS VANCE

A Message from the Chairman, John C. Whitehead

▶ ▶ ▶ ▶ ▶ ▶ ▶ ▶ ▶ ▶

Refugees are an important part of our nation's greatness. They make the best citizens because they know the value of freedom. I firmly believe this and am committed to working for their cause. It is this cause that gave rise to the International Rescue Committee sixty years ago, and IRC has remained devoted to refugees ever since.

Today we find ourselves in a "new world order." The end of the cold war has brought about a world safe at last from the threat of all-out nuclear warfare. But new and unexpected conflicts are breaking out all around the globe: in places such as former Yugoslavia, where ethnic animosities have exploded into chaotic slaughter; and in Somalia, where ancient clan divisions are destroying an entire country.

There are more refugees in the world today than ever before, and the issues of refugee relief are more complex than in the past. The challenge to IRC is to remain faithful to its mandate while adjusting to unparalleled crises. We must be vigilant and always at the vanguard of humanitarian response.

How will we keep ourselves ready? We must be always working to strengthen IRC's leadership capability. Headquarters must be as strong as it can be. A cadre of seasoned board members, field staff, and dedicated volunteers must be maintained and built upon. IRC is blessed with wonderful, capable people who are devoted to their work. This family must be kept together.

At a moment's notice a team of experts might be needed anywhere in the world. We must be ready for that eventuality. And because there are no standard solutions to the unprecedented crises of the modern age, IRC staff must be not only experienced but adaptable. Sometimes situations require us to act in entirely new ways. Innovation that emerges out of experience is what is required.

IRC will continue to grow in response to the challenges we face. Not for the sake of growth but because our services are more and more needed. We must continue to expand our resources and increase public awareness of our work.

What if IRC is forced to say no, unable to commit itself to responding to a particular emergency? How can we say yes to one crisis but no to another? What are the criteria that help us determine our course? First is the mandate that was the impulse for IRC's inception sixty years ago: to assist those forced to flee persecution. Political refugees terrorized because of race, religion, ethnicity, ideology, color, creed—all fall under the mandate of the International Rescue Committee. Once a refugee was someone who left his or her homeland and crossed a border to seek safety. Today there are thousands of refugees within the borders of a single nation—the internally displaced. What they need is what refugees have always needed: protection and care. And IRC is helping them. As the definition of a refugee evolves, so too does the work of IRC.

A very pressing issue today is security. There was a time when relief workers were relatively safe. But that is no longer the case. There is little regard in many places for the IRC insignia, or that of any other international relief agency. The issue of security will be with us for some time, and it is one that the IRC board of directors and staff must consider carefully with each decision to launch a program.

The availability of resources is also an important criterion in making programmatic decisions. IRC must be practical if it is to survive and thrive.

After six decades of dedicated service to refugees the International Rescue Committee is respected the world over. Today it is the leading nonsectarian agency devoted to the cause of refugees, highly regarded for its expertise and effectiveness.

What are the strengths that enable IRC to make such a singular contribution to humanitarian efforts? First is the agency's ability to act quickly. IRC has never been a ponderous, bureaucratic, or top-heavy organization. Programs emerge from the ground up, designed

in response to the crisis at hand to meet immediate needs. IRC has many times been the first voluntary agency on the scene of a refugee emergency. And IRC always hits the ground running. Work begins even as assessments are made. Reports and recommendations are fired back to headquarters, where the task of assembling necessary resources begins. All of this can happen in a matter of hours. And every hour makes a difference.

IRC is also adaptable. When it became clear that getting needed supplies into former Yugoslavia was an awesome if not impossible task, IRC was not stopped. We reopened local factories that are now producing coal stoves and plastic sheeting and other goods that are saving lives.

There is no work more important than that being done by the International Rescue Committee. And no one is doing it better. I have never been associated with an organization that does so much with so few resources. Every dollar is stretched to its fullest potential.

IRC has always been and remains a leader in refugee relief. We must always be at the vanguard of international responses to crises, rescuing lives and preserving freedom the world over.

John C. Whitehead

▶ ▶ ▶ ▶ ▶ ▶ ▶ ▶ ▶ ▶

We end where we began. Today IRC is in Europe, processing refugees for resettlement abroad. From an office in Zagreb, Croatia, IRC is assisting those uprooted by the violence in what was once Yugoslavia.

As always, the first cases to be considered are those of the most vulnerable: women, especially those who have been traumatized by rape and other forms of violence; children; ex-detainees; and Bosnian Muslims with family members already living in the United States. The stories told by those seeking safety are filled with terror and brutality almost beyond comprehension. But we know the stories are true, because they are repeated again and again. In many cases the stories are told by women with small children whose husbands have been killed or conscripted for fighting.

The task of the original volunteers who were the IRC was to rescue those targeted for death by the Gestapo. Today we are once again helping targets of ethnic cleansing to make their way to freedom, to begin life in a new land.

The publication of Flight *was made possible by generous gifts from Marvin Josephson and the late Harold Charno.*